T0147183

EDGE OF ETERNITY

IS DEATH REALLY THE END OF IT ALL?

VALENCIA MCMAHON

WESTBOW
PRESS®
A DIVISION OF THOMAS NELSON
& ZONDERVAN

WestBow Press books may be ordered through booksellers or by contacting:

WestBow Press
A Division of Thomas Nelson & Zondervan
1663 Liberty Drive
Bloomington, IN 47403
www.westbowpress.com
844-714-3454

ISBN: 978-1-6642-5019-2 (sc)
ISBN: 978-1-6642-5020-8 (hc)
ISBN: 978-1-6642-5018-5 (e)

Library of Congress Control Number: 2021923388

Print information available on the last page.

WestBow Press rev. date: 2/7/2022

CONTENTS

The Mattie Kemp Story

The Cash McMahon Story

Valencia's Testimony

Death is not the end for those who die in Jesus Christ. His promised return and the resurrection of the righteous will be realized at the appointed time.

ACKNOWLEDGMENTS

I was inspired to write this book when I realized just how much God loves me. After a night of despair when I lost my husband, clarity came in the morning. I had the opportunity to look back and see how God had allowed me to marry the man I said I would marry exactly ten years earlier. During my time of grief, I allowed myself to fall into the loving embrace of God's arms. It was He who sustained me during my losses.

I am grateful to have had the encouragement of my late husband's friends Alan S. Maltz, Erika King, William Fiore, and Marsha Jouben. I can see why they were special to him.

I'm also grateful to Javine Owens and Marilyn Oates, for encouraging me over this past year along with the rest of my friends and family who always provided valuable feedback when asked. Each of you helped make this book special.

DEDICATION

This book is dedicated to my mother, who taught me about the love of God since I was a child. To my sisters who thought the world of me, and to my loving husband who was always there for me with his beautiful smile and quiet strength. I thank God for their love

This book is also dedicated to my Lord and Savior Jesus Christ. Though much was taken from me, I know that so much more was given to me by the one who loves me the most.

Thank You, Jesus, for Your everlasting love.

INTRODUCTION

"And God shall wipe away all tears from their eyes; and there shall be no more death, neither sorrow, nor crying, neither shall there be any more pain: for the former things have passed away." After the fulfillment of the coming of the Messiah, His death, and His resurrection, no other Bible verse seems to compel the longing of the human heart as this one verse in Revelation 21:4 does. That glorious day is coming when we will no longer have to carry the burden of grief from losing our loved ones.

Grief is the one human emotion that all humanity will experience, whether from losing someone or something. It has made its way through the halls of history, and its presence is still here today in the year 2021. Imagine that thousands and thousands of years have gone by, and it is still hanging around. Many people have asked why. I would like to present to you another question: Why not? Grief is still around today because humanity is still around today.

The only place that suffering will no longer exist is in the new heaven and the new Earth God has promised to His people—that glorious place we read about in Revelation chapter 21. Imagine living in a place so beautiful, a place like nothing you have ever seen or experienced before. Imagine the Creator of the universe is there with us. If you can imagine it and believe in Him, the one who promised that to us will soon turn grief into joy.

Nothing can be more painful than the loss of a loved one. Equally so, nothing can be more life-changing than the loss of a loved one. I've experienced the loss of loved ones back-to-back on multiple occasions, and honestly, I've asked why many times. The question of why drove me to search for an answer. In my search, I found myself getting closer and closer to my Creator. So close until I started asking myself the question, "Why not?" Didn't God tell us that the wages of sin are death? And since all have sinned (Romans 3:23), then death is an unwelcome visitor that comes to us all. With the full knowledge that death is inevitable, then there must be a way for the human race to cope. Grief may be hard to picture as a gift because it's an emotion that none of us wants to have, yet it is a way to show the heights and depths of the love and appreciation we had for the ones we've lost. There is no doubt it will change you. But we get to decide whether that change will be for the better or it will make us bitter.

In every situation, we need to remember that God has assured us in His word that He will never leave us nor forsake us. As the psalmist said in Psalm 23:4, "Yea, though I walk through the valley of the shadow of death, I will fear no evil: for Thou art with me." Why is He with us? Because Psalm 23:1 says, "The Lord is my shepherd, I shall not want." The Lord is with us because He is our shepherd and our comforter. What does a good shepherd do? He guides his flock. He makes them lie down in green pastures. He leads them beside the still waters. He restores their souls. He leads them in paths of righteousness. And that is why the psalmist wrote in Psalm 30:5, "Weeping may endure for a night, but joy cometh in the morning." And when that joy comes, 'I will dwell in the house of the Lord forever" (Psalm 23:6).

As I journeyed through my losses, I found myself on an emotional roller-coaster ride that had me ready to give up on who and what I believed. It took the intervention of a loving God, who is still revealing Himself to me, to get me where I am today. It is that intervention that has me counting my blessings despite the losses. One of my favorite hymns by Thomas Shepherd asks the question, "Must Jesus bear the cross alone and all the world go free?" Then he answers, "No, there's a cross for everyone, and there's a cross for me"!

When heaped upon our weak, mortal bodies, the cross of grief is a load often too heavy to bear. But Jesus, who has gone down that road, is more than able to not only carry the load but take us through the grief. "My grace is sufficient for thee," He says in 2 Corinthians 12:9, "for my strength is made perfect in weakness."

We must hold fast to the hope and that blessed assurance that joy will indeed come in the morning. Joy will come, and we will once again enjoy the presence of our loved ones in our immortal bodies that Jesus Christ, the righteous, will give to all those who put their trust in Him. What a day of rejoicing that will be.

Unwillingly traveling down this lonely road called grief, I often wondered how long I would be in such a state. What I came to realize is that I would be in that state until I was no longer in that state. There is no set time frame when it comes to grieving. It simply takes as long as it takes. The depth of grief will depend on what was lost and your relationship to what was lost.

It is the resurrection that keeps me moving forward. Jesus is coming back to get His people from the ages of time! Even the angels testify to Jesus coming again. In Acts 1:11, the two angels who stood with the disciples as they watched Jesus ascend into heaven said, "Ye men of Galilee, why stand ye gazing up into heaven? This same Jesus which is taken up from you into heaven shall so come again in like manner as ye have seen him go into heaven." We find these words to be correct as Paul tells us in 1 Thessalonians 4:17. The righteous who are alive at the time of Jesus's second coming will be caught up in the air with the resurrected righteous dead at His second coming to meet Him in the clouds. We should remember that though all else may fail, we must hold fast to our faith and trust Jesus to keep His word.

So until that day, go ahead and grieve your loved ones. Our grief is a blessing from God, for it is a way for the body to heal itself. Embrace it with all of the love you had for your loved ones who are no longer with us. Never fear the tears—love works that way. Nevertheless, let us comfort one another and hold fast to the hope of the resurrection that He promised His people. Join me on my journey as I experience the painful depths of sorrow, only to find the pinnacle of eternal hope. Eternity is waiting.

FAITH WHEN ALL ELSE FAILS

Jesus said in Matthew 17:20 that if we had faith the size of a grain of mustard seed, we could move the mountains in our lives. Nothing would be impossible for us. When I think about that kind of faith, immediately two characters from the Bible come to mind, Noah and Abraham. These men showed faith when it did not make any sense to do so. God had told them something that not only seemed improbable but impossible as well. It had not rained before, so how would you destroy the world by a flood when there was not enough water to do so? How was Abraham to become the father of all nations if he sacrificed his seed—the seed through which those nations were to come? Neither man had the answers, but they both trusted God to do as He said. It was years before they saw God's promise come to pass. Just consider Noah, for over one hundred years building a massive ark on dry land, when there was no water even close to where he was. Talk about that grain of mustard seed. I can only say, what faith! Noah was looking forward to that blessed hope—the promise.

Today, we are still heirs to the promise that God made to Abraham, but do we believe that? Can our faith stand fast when the walls come crashing down around us? Can our faith stand when the Lord gives and the Lord takes away? Will our walk with Jesus match our lip service? I was sure I believed in Jesus with all my heart, and I felt my faith could withstand any test. What I did not know then was that God would put my faith to the test. I would see my faith tested in the coming weeks as I had never seen it tried before.

When you look at the Bible's account of what faith is, it is first and foremost a gift from God. Faith is neither earned nor bought. In Hebrews 11:1, Paul tells us that "faith is the substance of things hoped for, the evidence of things not seen." You might ask, "What exactly does that mean?" Faith is what brings things that are not yet seen but hoped for into our lives. Faith is trusting in God to do all that He said He would do, not all that we ask Him to do. Throughout history, countless prayer requests have gone from the lips of humankind to the ears of God. We believe that when asked, God will answer our requests. For those of us whose faith does much abound, we move forward knowing that we've already received what we prayed about. Genesis 15:6, Romans 4:3, and Galatians 3:6 all say Abraham believed God, and it was counted to him as righteousness.

But that was then. What about now, in the year 2021? What happens when our prayers are not answered the way we hoped? Can faith still exist among God's people? *What about me? Could I be a modern-day Noah or Abraham and simply have faith in God? What happens if my prayers don't get answered, as I believed they would? Does my faith hold firm? Like Noah and Abraham, will I blindly follow God, trusting that He has a plan for every little thing coming my way?* Having grown up in the church, I was about to discover if I am who I say I am.

THE PYTRISHA HADDLY STORY

GOD CAN FIX IT

It was summer 2014 when I received a call from my niece informing me that my oldest sister, Pytrisha, her mother, was diagnosed with stage 4 ovarian cancer. I couldn't believe my ears. *How can this be?* I thought. My sister was always going to the doctor to get her regular checkups. "Surely there must be a mistake," I said, but my niece assured me that the doctor had confirmed the diagnosis.

When my niece asked the doctor why cancer had not been detected in any of her mother's checkups, he explained that ovarian cancer is sometimes not easily detected until the later stage. Needless to say, that answer did not sit well with us. I was overcome by sadness, and the tears were streaming steadily down my face. Immediately I thought God could fix this, so I prayed and asked God not to take my sister away. With my mother being diagnosed with Alzheimer's years before, my oldest sister was the glue that held the family together. What would we do without her? Due to the late stage of the disease, the doctor suggested chemotherapy treatments start right away.

I was not living in Florida at the time, so I couldn't physically be there with my sister. But I remember talking with her often on the phone. I knew her well, so I knew that she must have been thinking about who was going to take care of our mother if she did not survive. I could always tell how she was feeling by the sound of her voice, which was why I wanted to hear her voice as often as I could. I especially wanted to know where she was in her spiritual life since my mother had raised us in a Christian home. Something inside me knew that if she was okay spiritually, then we could get through this.

I had not received any assurances from God personally; however, I just decided to function as though He would heal her. After all, He is the God of miracles, and I had my faith.

When asked, she always said she was okay. I didn't worry much because she always sounded solid and sure. I often talked with my sister about her faith in God. She never gave up on her faith, so I used that for my comfort. "Lord, if You don't heal her, help us to accept Your will." The words came out of my mouth, though I'm not so sure my heart was ready to face that possibility of God not healing her. The hope in me was still there, so I chose to have faith. I just kept praying for her healing. I was confident that God would do so. It was a better reality for me, so I focused on that. I did not allow myself to think about my sister dying. Psalm 91 was one of her favorite Psalms, and that was great because it has always been one of my favorites. It always gave me strength during the times when I had none. And that had become often. .

> He that dwelleth in the secret place of the most High shall abide under the shadow of the Almighty. I will say of the Lord, He is my refuge and my fortress: my God; in him will I trust. (Psalm 91:1–2)

At the time, I did not know that death would weave its cruel and destructive way into my life and inflict the most unbearable pain on my heart. The devil himself was coming to wage war against a child of God. Ready or not, my faith was about to be tested. Some may think that I was burying my head in the sand. The chances of survival with stage 4 cancers were nearly none to impossible. I did trust God to be her refuge, to be the God who heals. Her healing would take a miracle. I knew a God who specializes in those miracles all the time. Why couldn't my sister be one of those miracles? For months the chemo treatment continued, but after the first year, her health started to decline. She was getting sicker and sicker with each treatment. She was relentless, though. I don't know how she could do it, but she still found the strength to take care of our mother. They had a special bond and she was not ready to give up yet.

I tell you, there is a God in heaven, and He rules in the affairs of men. Oh, how sweet the words written by Thomas Moore: "Come, ye disconsolate, wherever ye languish: earth has no sorrow that heaven cannot heal." There was plenty of sorrow that I needed heaven to heal. For my sister, though, I wanted to be as strong for her as she always sounded. The psalmist David said:

> I will lift up mine eyes unto the hills, from whence cometh my help. My help cometh from the LORD, which made heaven and earth. (Psalm 121:1–2)

My sister loved that bible verse. I'm sure that it was by the grace of God that we both received our strength each day. I was able to speak with her weekly to encourage her. We encouraged each other. I can't tell you how much good it did my heart and faith to know that her trust in God, her Creator, remained firm. She knew that even if she did not survive this, she would reap the reward of eternal life in the resurrection. I believed that as well. That still in no way meant that I was ready to lose my big sister. Nothing could be further from the truth.

During the second year, when her health declined even further, she started to need assistance with her own daily needs, so my niece Robin started going over each day to assist her and my mother. I could not transfer home at that time due to my work, so I was still not physically able to help. I happily did what I could from afar. On the occasions that she needed to go to her doctor's appointment, my ex-sister-in-law would come over to watch my mother. At other times, my middle sister Linda or one of my brother's would go over to attend to my mother.

HOMECOMING

It was September of 2015 when I was able to come back home again for vacation. I was so excited to be going home to visit my sisters and mother. When I walked in the door, I immediately noticed my sister had lost a lot of weight. My heart quickened, and my countenance fell within me. But all they saw was my smile that I hoped showed in my eyes. She was a tiny little thing, but she still had spirit. We greeted each other with a huge embrace as usual.

I remember that her grip was much tighter this time, though. It was as if she was hugging me for the last time, in case she did not get to see me again. I spent as much time with them as I could before heading back to Atlanta. We laughed and talked for hours about all of the good times we had enjoyed through the years. My mother was always there, but she could not coherently join the conversation because of her advanced stage of Alzheimer's. That didn't stop her from making gestures that let us know she was still with us. Those were my fondest memories of the four of us being together. We were still the four golden girls, though two of us had been married.

After I flew back home to Atlanta, I would still talk to my sister on the phone for weeks. She was always very upbeat. That's how she was the last time I spoke with her. Shortly after I returned home, my sister's chemo treatment had stopped. The cancer had spread throughout her frail body. Because of that, they kept her sedated so she wouldn't feel the pain that coursed through her body. One day I received the dreaded call that she had gone into hospice. My heart started racing, trying to keep up with my thoughts that were spiraling out of control. God give me strength.

Disappointed and saddened by the news, I made my decision. I was moving back to my childhood home once I sold the house in Atlanta, even if I didn't have a job. The good news was that God was working behind the scenes. I found out that I had received approval from management to transfer to Florida and work out of the corporate office there. It didn't matter at that point, though, because I was moving back home. I was needed there very much.

During the Christmas break, I was heading home to visit family once again. I remember I felt a strange feeling that I can't explain to this day. At the last minute, I decided to contact the airlines to see if I could fly out at least one day earlier than my scheduled flight. Later I learned that things had become worse for my sister. I needed to be there to see her one last time before she took her last breath. Could it be that God had put that thought in my mind? As I look back now, I'm convinced that He did.

GOD'S GONE AND DONE IT

I arrived at the Fort Lauderdale airport on December 19, 2015. It was almost a week before Christmas. I was late getting in due to some significant delays flying out of Atlanta. I had missed two earlier flights through no fault of my own, so I was not in the best of moods. Once I was in the baggage claim area, I called my niece to let her know that I had finally arrived and would be at the hospital to visit with my sister as soon as possible.

I gave the representative my name and ID to collect my baggage that had arrived on an earlier flight when I heard my niece say, "Auntie, Mommy passed." Due to the noise in the airport, I wasn't sure I'd heard what I thought I heard, so I said, "What?" She repeated those awful words. Shocked with disbelief, I didn't have any comments. Tears rolled down my face. I was too late. A range of emotions went through me all at once. At first, I thought if only there hadn't been such a delay at the Atlanta airport, I would have made it to the hospital in time. It made me angry, and I wanted to scream. I couldn't scream, though. I was in the middle of the Fort Lauderdale airport. So I simply held the pain in and quietly let the tears flow. My sister was gone, and there was nothing I could do.

The realization of what the doctor had said in 2014 had come true. She had passed within the two years. I waited outside for Cash, my significant other at the time, to pick me up. Cash arrived, and he helped me into the car. With tears still streaming down my face, I told him what had happened. We drove to the hospital in silence. I kept beating myself up mentally about not being there. I was supposed to have been there. She was my sister. There was no miracle for my sister. I just sat there and cried. He quietly held my hand as we drove the rest of the way in silence. He was always my quiet strength.

Even though I did not get the miracle I was hoping and praying for, I never once lost my faith. I had asked God, in the beginning, to help us be content with whatever the outcome would be. I closed my eyes and repeated Matthew 6:10, "Thy kingdom come, thy will be done in earth as it is in heaven." Now I don't believe that God's will was that my sister should die, but I understood that her death did not go unnoticed by Him. Nevertheless, she was gone, and there was no changing that. Now, I had to wrestle with my emotions. I have to look forward to that blessed hope of the resurrection.

When we arrived at the hospital, I saw my nephew in the hallway and asked where my sister was. He pointed to the room down the hall. As I continued walking toward the room, I reflected that he would not hear her call him Darling anymore. I looked inside the room, but I did not see my sister, so I went on walking to the next room. I saw my family members, but not her. *Indeed, she has to be here,* I thought.

I walked down the hall, but I didn't see my sister in any of the rooms. Finally, I went back to the room where my other family members were and asked my niece where my sister was. She replied, "Right here, Auntie," and then she moved out of the way. There was my sister, lying on the hospital bed, lifeless. I did not recognize her. She was smaller than the last time I had seen her. Her body was limp and frail, almost skeleton-like.

Immediately my mind flashed back over the years. I remembered my sister was tall, strong, vibrant, and full of life, though the last time I saw her she had lost a lot of weight. She was my big sister, and just like that, she was gone from my life. She was gone from all of our lives. It wasn't the first time we had lost a sibling. One of my brothers, who lived in Detroit, had passed away years before. He was my brother, and I loved him, but his death did not affect me the same way. I guess it was because he did not grow up with me. It was different this time. I grew up with my sister always being a part of my life. My mother only had three daughters, and we were all close. Mentally, I asked God to give me strength, and I moved forward as though I already had it.

I'LL SEE YOU AGAIN

On December 29, 2015, we buried my sister where her husband was already lying at rest. It was the saddest day of my life. You couldn't tell from the outside, but on the inside, I felt as though the sadness would choke the very life out of me. Though I was sad, I felt a sense of relief. I knew where my sister had placed her trust. The thought of that is what brought about the comfort. My sister was gone, but God was still with me. I knew He wouldn't leave me at such a time as this.

> Do not be afraid; do not be discouraged, for the Lord your God will be with you wherever you go. (Joshua 1:9 NIV)

Imagine that—God is with me wherever I go. *Does that mean the grave as well?* I wondered. I remembered some of the words from a sermon I heard during my youth. The pastor talked about a Bible verse that mentions that very thing. God is with us wherever we go. I did not remember all the words, but I was determined to find the Bible verse. I searched on the Internet and found the words of the psalmist David: "'If I ascend up into heaven, thou art there: if I make my bed in hell, behold thou art there" (Psalm 139:8).

I had my answer. If the love of God is with us when we are riding high, so to speak, and all is well, then indeed the love of God is with us when we breathe our last breath. When our bodies are resting in their graves, He loves us still, even in death. How very comforting to know.

My mother was there with us that day as we held the funeral service for her eldest daughter. I was looking at her, intensely studying her facial expressions. I wondered how she would react to what was going on. It was her eldest daughter, the one who had been by her side taking care of her for the past several years. I had a flashback and recalled for a brief moment my mother often calling my middle sister or me Ann. That was my oldest sister's middle name. In my mind, I just smiled and watched my mother for a long time, waiting for her to break down. She never did. She sat there quietly in her wheelchair as the service went on. What a blessing! While it may sound strange, I felt as if God was there, comforting my mother, and I was glad. I was pleased because I did not want to see her display the pain of losing her daughter.

If I'm sincere, I was glad because I did not want the pain of seeing my mother's pain, fearing I would not be able to comfort her. It felt good to believe that Alzheimer's had progressed to such a degree that she did not wholly understand what was happening that day—the permanence of it. Though she could not tell us how she felt, she did turn to me and point toward my sister. She knew it was her daughter who was lying there. I chose to be content with thinking she did not fully understand that she would not see Pytrisha, her eldest daughter again in this life.

At the service, I talked about my sister. I spoke about the ten children my mother had, but of the ten, only three were girls. That meant I only had one sister left. I had made a point of that fact as I looked at my new oldest sister and continued to speak. I knew that no matter how tough things would be, one day, the three of us would be okay again. The infamous four golden girls were now just three. We were still all for one and one for all. We said our goodbyes at the gravesite and went back to the family home. I remember thinking about heaven that day. It's a place I certainly want to find myself in at the end of this life. I am planning on seeing my sister again there as well. For now, she would lie in her grave with her husband until the resurrection. I was content with that.

As we gathered at the family house afterward, we reminisced about the good times we had at my sister's place. The holidays were excellent times. It was like having Sunday dinner at a comedy club.

The stories she would often share with us were informative and funny. Once my sister told us the most amusing story when one of our younger brothers picked her up from the grocery store. She said his driving was so awful that when they finally arrived home alive, with legs trembling, the fear of death on her face, she quickly got out of the car and left all of her groceries in the car. She was so thankful to make it home alive. It was more amusing to me because I had had the same unfortunate occasion to have him give me a ride to my car. Like my sister, I, too, was thankful to step out of his car alive.

Ah, the food! My mind drifted, and my mouth began to water as I remembered the cornbread patties she used to make. Those patties were the best. My sister took to cooking after my mom. Not me; I didn't get that talent, and it didn't bother me in the least.

Life changed for me that day. It had changed for all of us. And though I was not sure what the future held for me, I knew that I would not be alone. Jesus promised never to leave me nor forsake me. For as long as I live, I will not only hold on to that promise, but I will hold Jesus to that promise. I know my sister's faith and trust were not in vain. Neither is mine. When I meditate on it, I can see the resurrection in my mind. So, like the apostle Paul, I can boldly say, "I know whom I have believed and am persuaded that he is able to keep that which I have committed unto him against that day" (2 Timothy 1:12).

A MIND AT REST

It wasn't until later that Cash showed me a picture he had taken. It was a beautiful moment that he had captured on his camera. There we were, in perfect order. It could not have been planned any better if we had tried. It was my new oldest sister, me, my niece, my great-niece, and my great-great-niece all looking down at the sister, mother, grandmother, and great-grandmother we had lost. Four generations gathered at that moment in time. I remember smiling at him and putting my head on his shoulder as I cried. Who was this man in my life? He had kept quiet in the background, watching, waiting. When he had seen us standing there together, he instinctively knew that it was a moment he wanted to capture for us—for me. Cash's actions in that situation were one of the reasons I loved him.

Again I remembered that I hadn't gotten my miracle, but I didn't lose my faith that day. I was hurting badly, and I needed spiritual strength, so I went to God's word. It had not failed me yet, and now was not going to be any different.

> For the wages of sin is death; but the gift of God is eternal life through Jesus Christ our Lord. (Romans 6:23)

> Thou wilt keep him in perfect peace whose mind is stayed on thee: because he trusteth in thee. (Isaiah 26:3)

Because of the faith and trust that I still have in God, I had the strength to endure. I trust God's promises. I believe that all of God's children can agree that receiving the gift of eternal life is worth the crosses we bear. I am reminded once again of the song we used to sing growing up in church: "Must Jesus bear the cross alone, and all the world go free? No, there's a cross for everyone, and there's a cross for me." Life, death, and eternity; it's all a part of God's plan of redemption. I won't tell you that my mind comes anywhere near comprehending God's timeline in regard to Jesus's coming to take His people back home. I won't tell you because I don't understand it. When I sometimes think about eternity, it makes my head spin. What I do know is that I believe. With all that God has shown us, shown me—with all that I have read in His word—how could I not believe? Jesus said in John 14:1–3,

> Let not your heart be troubled: ye believe in God, believe also in me. In my father's house are many mansions: if it were not so, I would have told you. I go to prepare a place for you. And if I go and prepare a place for you, I will come again, and receive you unto myself; that where I am, there ye may be also.

My sister is now resting and waiting. These words will reside in my heart permanently as I continue to have faith and look forward to the resurrection.

Edge of Eternity

I Will Trust Thee, O My Father

I will trust Thee, O my Father,
For Thy love shall never fail;
In Thy arms I rest forever,
Safe within the second veil.
Thee I trust for every blessing,
All I need is in Thy will;
On Thy promise calmly resting,
Thou dost every want fulfill.
I will trust Thee, fearing never,
All my doubts have fled away;
In my Jesus trusting ever,
I abide in perfect day.
I will trust in every trial,
In Thy providence confide;
Thou art with me in the furnace,
Thou art ever by my side.

—Clarence E. Hunter

The Gift

The gift of God is eternal life, through Jesus
Christ, His Son
A gift so rare yet open to all, the victory
already won
It cannot be claimed by the works of man,
for no one's heart is pure
It's Calvary alone, the sacrifice there, that only
will endure
Christ died to save the human race, which was
His Father's plan
The choice is yours, the time is now, choose wisely
if you can.

—Valencia McMahon

SILENCE IS NOT GOLDEN

Earlier, we talked about faith when all else fails. But what is faith? Is it something we all have in varying degrees, or is it something you either have or don't have? If it's in varying degrees, then I certainly had faith, I thought. If it's something you either have or don't have, I fell into that category also. I was sure I knew what I believed. I couldn't think of anything that could threaten that belief.

Like the startling crack of lightning flashing across the sky, tragedy was about to strike again unexpectedly. I couldn't figure out what was going on, and when I asked God, His silence stunned me. I knew He was there, and I know He heard me, so why the silence? Was He just going to leave me hanging on a wing and a prayer?

Often when things don't go our way, we decide to take out our frustration on God. We fool ourselves into thinking that we can punish God by our behavior. So we go on strike. We stop going to church; we stop doing the little good we are capable of doing. Even worse, we stop praying. We go silent, trying to mimic God in what we perceive as silence on His part. We forget that God's ways are not our ways, and His thoughts are not our thoughts.

What I came to realize in time is that God was never silent. He was speaking to me in the things happening in, around, and through me. It was my ears that could not hear. They could not hear because I was focusing on my broken heart. I couldn't see how my broken heart was going to mend, no matter how much faith I had.

I would have never imagined what was looming just a few days around the corner. It was unthinkable. Ignorance is bliss, someone once said, and indeed it is. I didn't know what was coming my way, but I'd soon find out that faith—my faith—was about to be tested again. If I thought the first time was something, then indeed, what was ahead was something altogether different and far beyond what I had imagined. I went silent for a long time, not able to find any words to communicate with God. One could imagine that my faith was dead.

The Four Seasons wrote the song "Silence is Golden," and it became trendy back in the 1960s. But I found out that silence is never golden when that silence keeps you from communicating with God—the source of all our help and strength.

THE LINDA GOLDEN STORY

A SMILE AT MIDNIGHT

I was always close to my sisters, but I was incredibly close to my middle sister Linda. She and my niece spent countless weekends at my house. If we weren't out shopping, we'd be at the house talking, laughing, and pampering ourselves. It didn't matter what we did, as long as we did it together. And though the trip home in December 2015 was not a happy one due to the circumstances of my visit, we still found time for the three of us to get together.

I have to admit that this time was not like all the times in the past. How could it be? This time instead of laughing, talking, and pampering ourselves, we shared memories of Pytrisha my oldest sister. We talked about all the good times we had had together. All the family holiday get-togethers at her place or my mother's place. The songs she loved, our favorite foods she used to cook. It was odd, but we did manage to laugh a little at some of the memories.

We talked about her selfless act of moving from her place to my mother's to take care of her full-time when my mother was diagnosed with Alzheimer's. We talked about how she continued to take care of my mother after my sister was diagnosed with cancer. She touched all of our lives. I don't think my middle sister was quite ready to be the big sister, but that was our new reality. Living that new reality was almost unthinkable.

Later I dropped them both off at home, and then I headed back to the beach where I always stayed when I was in town. I don't remember if we spoke on Thursday, which was New Year's Eve, but I remember Friday, January 1, 2016, because it was my nieces' birthday. I called them to see if they wanted to celebrate before I flew back to Atlanta the next day. I didn't get a call back from my sister until January 2, the day I was leaving. We were excited to talk about me finally moving back home by that summer. That made her happy, and so I was delighted as well. I could tell she missed me being within a short driving distance.

During our conversation, she let on that she was worried about some things—the car that always gave her trouble, the job that she didn't quite like at times, not having enough money to pay all her bills, and so on. Her worries were about things that many people struggle with every day. She didn't want to come to me for assistance this time. She was determined to make it on her own somehow. She had her pride, and I didn't want to push.

As I look back on that particular day, I don't know why, but she was more stressed than she's ever been as long as I've known her. I would always tell her as I did that day not to stress about things too much. "Stress can kill you," I would always say. She always responded, "Yeah, I know." She knew it well enough, but that didn't stop the roller-coaster ride of stress that seemingly dominated her life. It seemed to be on the downward path with a few loops but no sign of going up.

In an attempt to bring her out of her state of stress, I reminded her again that I would be back home by the coming summer, and we could go back to hanging out like old times. Not only was she excited about that, but also she was happy that Cash and I were back together. After our usual long conversation, she had some things that she wanted to do, so I told her I would let them know when I arrived at the airport, and then I hung up.

Once I had checked in at the Fort Lauderdale airport, I did what I always did when I traveled. I sent a text message to everyone to give an update on my status. This time I added the picture that Cash had taken of us at my sister's grave. They all thought it was beautiful. The last text I received back was from my sister Linda, and her reply was just one word: "Nice." I didn't arrive in Atlanta until late that evening. I sent them a text saying that I had landed in Atlanta and that I was on the train heading to my car. I didn't get a response. I didn't expect one. It was late after all, going on midnight. I remember smiling as I thought to myself that everyone was sleeping at that hour. For sure they would all see it when they awoke in the daylight hours.

OH NO, HE DIDN'T

It was January 3, 2016, when I awoke to a new day. Though I had to swallow the bitter pill with the loss of my oldest sister, I was thankful to have my middle sister. I allowed myself to feel the excitement of moving back home, so I went out and did a little shopping. It was shortly after 5:00 p.m. on January 3, 2016, when I arrived back home.

I was laying the bags on the kitchen counter when my cell phone rang. It was a call from my niece. I thought she was calling me to talk since we hadn't had the chance to speak before I left Miami. Nothing in my life or even in this world had prepared me for what I heard next. "Hello," I said, and I listened to her voice quivering as if she had been crying.

"Auntie, Auntie Linda is dead." There was only silence for a moment. I had heard similar words only days before, but I was sure I must have heard the wrong thing. "Auntie Linda is dead," she said again. Stunned, I still didn't know what to say. I didn't even know what to feel.

There was a range of emotions going through me. I had just buried my oldest sister on December 29, 2015, and now this! What was this ungodly nightmare I just got plunged into? My only sister left was now dead. *How can that be?* I remembered my comment last night about everyone sleeping. They were, but everyone woke up the next day except for my sister.

Immediately I asked God why. My heart was aching. "Why would You do this to me?" She was the only sister I had left. I sobbed uncontrollably. I could accept that I did not get the miracle with my eldest sister, but this was too much to bear. It was way too much to take in five days.

I was finally able to ask what had happened, and she went on to explain that my nephew, her eldest son, after getting a call from his younger brother about not being able to reach their mother, went over to check on her. He had tried earlier but did not get an answer either, which is why he went over.

My sister usually spoke with both her sons every day, so naturally, the younger one called his big brother when she did not answer. Thankfully my nephew happened to be down in the area, so it didn't take him long to get to her house. When he went inside, he discovered his mother's body, lying on her bed alone. She was locked away in a place that had become her tomb.

My heart ached even more for him. I would have given anything for him not to be the one who found his mother's body that way—alone behind locked doors. The cause of her death was unknown.

When I hung up the phone, I was terrified to leave the house. Death had invaded my thoughts, and I thought it would surely come for me next. In my family room, there I stood, a woman who only five days ago still declared her faith in God, after burying her oldest sister. Now I was hearing that my remaining sister was gone. She was gone from my life as well.

ELIJAH MOMENT

I was due back to work the next day, but there was no way I was going out that door. I remember calling my manager to share what had happened. I was nervously pacing the floor, trying to figure things out. Suddenly it occurred to me that my sister was inside the house when she died. Staying home was in no way a guarantee of my safety. I didn't care, though. I was terrified, and I wasn't going out that door, period.

Oddly, I thought this was the first time I had ever known real fear. I felt like Elijah when Jezebel was killing all the prophets. He ran for his life and hid. He had seen God rain down fire from heaven to prove that He was the living God, yet Elijah still feared for his life when it was under threat.

No Bible verses came to mind to offer any comfort this time. There was no raining fire down from heaven moment for me. There was just death. And death, it seemed, was at my door. This time I thought God had left me. I didn't know why God decided to go, but I was sure He had left me. I was full of fear, full of sadness and anger; I didn't even know how to pray then. I was bitterly disappointed.

I called Cash to let him know what had happened. He was always my rock. This time he was not close by to offer his strength, but I knew his heart went out to me. Later that evening, my manager at the time and a coworker came over to sit with me. I knew I had to fly back home, but I stayed on that couch for two days and two nights with no sleep. I didn't want to sleep, fearing I would not wake up again. There were no prayers from my lips those nights. I did not say a single verse of scripture to comfort me.

My manager stayed at my house for two nights. One of my coworkers came over to the house during the daytime and worked there so I would not be home alone. God wasn't on the scene, I thought, but I had two people close by who were.

By midweek, I had made arrangements to fly back home on Wednesday, January 6. It was a horrible flight, filled with agonizing fear that paralyzed me the entire time. I can't say that I had faith at the time, but I remember that I kept praying all the way, and I kept hoping for the best. They say that flying is the safest way to travel, so I was banking on that more than I was on my faith.

Again, Cash picked me up from the airport. He embraced me and said, "I'm sorry." There were no other words to say. As always, he quietly held my hand, only a little tighter this time as if he was giving me all his strength. I needed it. I wasn't afraid when I was with him. I knew he would protect me. For a moment, I wanted to believe that God was still with me because I needed that assurance. I couldn't feel him, though. I only felt the pain from the loss of my dear sister, whom I loved very much.

WEIGHING IN THE BALANCE

On the drive back to the beach, I remember thinking, *Why would God allow such a thing?* This was cruel beyond measure. Didn't He know my sister and I were very close? Didn't He know we had plans to carry out once I moved back home? Didn't He know I was looking forward to those plans?

I closed my eyes and let all the memories of us growing up together flood my mind. It was pain and pleasure at the same time. The pain was from knowing we would not have those times again. After I moved to Georgia, we still talked every day on our way to or from work. We couldn't hang out as we had before, but we still talked every day.

It wasn't until later that Cash and I met up with some of the family members. If I thought burying my oldest sister was hard, then this was going to be almost impossible. Still there were no Bible verses that came to mind for comfort. I was struggling. I tried to pull from everything in my background of faith, everything I had learned from childhood until then. Nothing came to me. All I had were questions, with not even one acceptable answer. Just like a whisper on a quiet summer's night, my faith was gone with the wind.

I took on the task of finding the clothes for my sister to wear during her funeral service. While that was a task I would not put on anyone, it was still an honor despite the screaming inside my head. I didn't have the courage required, let alone the strength, but I was going to do it. My sister rarely wore anything other than jeans and

T-shirts, so to find something to dress her in for the service was going to be a real challenge.

The next day I went looking with my niece, but we didn't find anything so the following day I went shopping alone. I remembered I had been in that store before with my sister. It was a horrible experience this time, and I hated it. I felt sick to my stomach. After I dropped the clothes off at the funeral home and told them how to style her hair, I headed back to the house on the beach. All I could think was that I needed Cash's strength.

On the way back, alone with my thoughts, all I could do was ask what could have happened. My sister was not sick. It had been several days, and God still had not provided any comfort from His word for me. With a sarcastic chuckle, I told myself I didn't need His comfort. I was going to someone who would comfort me. I started to remember our last conversation. She was anxious and upset about the issues she was having with her car, about not being able to reach the mechanic, school was starting on Monday, and she needed the car. She was low on cash, and a host of other issues had her all stressed out. "Stress can kill you, you know," I would always say, and her reply was always "Yeah, I know."

Friday evening, January 8, 2016, had finally come, and we headed to the wake. That evening would be the first time I had seen my sister since December 30, the day after my oldest sister's funeral. I was still feeling those raw emotions when I opened the door to the church. There up ahead was my last sister. It felt as if I was walking down the aisle in the twilight zone. She was lying there, still as if she was sleeping at first glance. I wanted her to wake up. I needed her to wake up, but she didn't. I walked forward, but I wasn't ready to approach the casket just yet, so I sat on the front pew and just looked at her, desperately trying to figure out how she ended up there.

Still no Bible verses came to comfort me. It hurt too much to think, so I just stopped trying. I would let the pain engulf me. Finally, I walked up to the casket and stared down at her. There were other people in the church, but it only felt like the two of us. There are no words that I can say to express what was going through my mind. I felt angry, hurt, betrayed, and dismayed. It was a host of emotions that had nothing to do with being happy or having faith. Those emotions had nothing to do with understanding why on the following day I would be burying my last sister mere days after burying the first one.

I had no idea where God was, but I knew He wasn't with me anymore. I wondered what I had done wrong for Him to allow this to happen to me. Shouldn't a person be allowed to mourn the loss of a loved one entirely before they are hit again with such a painful loss? Death wasn't an accident after which you spend time in the hospital and then go home for recovery. It was permanent, and there was no coming back. This time I didn't think about the glory of the promised resurrection. Mine was faith broken by love.

Afterward, I went outside to get some fresh air. I needed to get away. I mingled and talked with other people, but it was superficial. People would always say that God is in control and that God knows best. I had once known that. Now it seemed there was no control in this random chaos. All I could think that night was *Why did God allow my sister to die alone?*

I wrestled back the tears. I could only hope that my sister was not afraid. Somehow I felt that I had let my sister down. I felt as if there was something more that I should have done to ease the stress she felt when I spoke with her. I didn't realize how bad it was, but I should have. After all, she was my sister. She was the last sister I had.

I should have found some comfort in knowing that I was the last person she had spoken with, but I didn't. As Cash and I drove back to the beach that night, I knew that I had to pull myself together for my two nephews' sake. They had enough grief to bear, so the last thing they would need was an aunt who had fallen apart. I needed to step up and be an adult. To do that, though, I needed something big from a God I felt had left me. It didn't matter whether I believed it or not at the time; I just needed some comforting words to say to them.

Sarcastically I thought, *Comforting words—is there such a thing in times like these?* If I had to cast a vote right then, I would vote an unequivocal no. Nevertheless, I needed to find some comforting words to say the following day at my sister's funeral service.

THINK ON THESE WORDS

I woke up Saturday morning, January 9, 2016, with a giant headache. I had had a long rough night but was finally able to get a few hours of sleep. I must have tried a thousand times to come up with some comforting words during my sleepless hours, but the words wouldn't come.

God must have seen my broken heart and taken pity on me because a familiar Bible verse came to me when I awoke. It was the Bible verse that one of my church sisters sent me when I lost my first sister. I spent time that morning thinking about all the good times we used to have together, all the good times we would never have together again, and I just wept. I wept long and hard in the arms of the man who loved me with all of his heart.

The time to leave was fast approaching, and like it or not, I had to attend my last sister's funeral service. We arrived at the church and greeted the long line of people going inside. There were people I knew and people I didn't know. Inside, the church was full of people. Her coworker's from the school where she worked were in attendance, and so was the school's principal. We took a seat on about the fourth row of the center aisle. One of my brothers came up with my mother and sat next to me. I noticed that my oldest brother, who was still in town, did not show up. I filed that away. These were terrible times, and Lord knows I was more than sick of them.

As the service progressed, songs were sung, and various people stood up to speak. It was all just a blur at the time. Then it was my turn. I stood up to take what seemed like the longest walk of my life.

All eyes were on me, the baby sister. I glanced over at my sister; she was in the same position I had seen her in the night before. I stood at the podium and looked out at the people.

If I could have had a superpower at that moment, it would have been invisibility because I just wanted to disappear. I wanted to be anywhere but standing there at that time. I stood there, though, silent at first. All eyes were on me waiting for me, the churchgoing, Bible-carrying, always-looking-on-the-bright-side-of-things baby sister, to say some words of profound wisdom that they could reflect on. I had nothing! I felt nothing but a deep sense of utter loss in a world where chaos ruled the day.

To save face and make the family proud, I thanked everyone for coming. I don't remember moving my lips, but the words did come out. I do remember saying to Brian and Tristian that their mother loved them both dearly. I talked about some of the good times I shared with my sister and how I would miss those times. I desperately wanted to cry, but there were words I needed to say, so I continued. Always the strong one I was.

In the end, I read the Bible verse that had come to me, hoping to give them comfort though I had none.

> But I would not have you to be ignorant, brethren, concerning them which are asleep, that ye sorrow not, even as others which have no hope. For if we believe that Jesus died and rose gain, even so them also which sleep in Jesus will God bring with him. For this we say unto you by the word of the Lord, that we which are alive and remain until the coming of the Lord shall not prevent them which are asleep. For the Lord himself shall descend from heaven with a shout, with the voice of the archangel, and with the trumpet of God: and the dead in Christ shall rise first. (1 Thessalonians 4:13–16)

I wanted them to know that day, at that moment, there was hope. I wanted them to know that they would see their mother again.

Looking back, I think I needed to believe that more than I needed them to believe it. But I didn't. When I finished, somehow I managed to focus on Cash, and my legs found the strength to walk back to my seat. The service proceeded. When the time came for the viewing of the body one last time, I sat still and watched as each person took their turn saying goodbye before the casket was closed forever. I rubbed my brother's back, trying to provide what little comfort I could. I looked over at my mother once again, hoping that she was not fully comprehending what was going on. If the first funeral service didn't break her, I thought undoubtedly another one so close together would do the job. She just sat there quietly in her wheelchair and watched.

Again I thought, *Well, at least Alzheimer's is good for something.* I had to be thankful for that. When it came time for our row, I stood up and walked up with the others. I looked at her casket for a few moments, telling myself, *This can't be real*—that it was a bad dream, and I wanted to wake up. It wasn't a bad dream, and I was already up. So with the *Twilight Zone* music playing in my head, I kissed my sister on the forehead and walked back to my seat.

When it came to the immediate family's turn, I intently watched my nephews, hoping they would have strength. I knew they must have been dying inside, so I was hoping that they kept their heavy emotions in check during that time. I was in no way ready to have an emotional breakdown just yet. I was not ready to have an emotional breakdown ever.

At the place where we laid her body to rest, the Pastor said the final words and the final prayer. Lovingly, we laid our flowers on her casket before the casket was placed inside the vault on the wall. It was over. Family and friends hugged each other and went their separate ways.

A SISTER'S CRY

Cash and I were the only two left after everyone else had gone. I couldn't bring myself to leave just yet. There I stood, alone, looking at this massive cold wall that housed the vault that would forever separate me from my sister. I looked up and saw Cash still waiting for me in the car. I stood there leaning against that cold wall, still holding a few of the flowers that I had taken from the baskets, talking to my sister. I don't remember what I said, and I knew she couldn't hear me anyway. But I still needed to say something, so I did.

I had stood there for a while before I turned to look at Cash again. I knew I had to leave, but I couldn't bring myself to do so. I knew that once I left, I would never go back. I whispered the words *I'm going to miss you* to my sister. Then I turned with tears in my eyes and walked to the car, and we left. That was the second-longest walk in my life to date.

As we drove off, I thought to myself, *Another sister resting for what happens next.* There was no gathering at the family home. I called my niece to see how she was doing. She was part of the trio that always hung out together on the weekends at my house. I figured she would need someone to talk to. Cash and I went to pick her up, and we took her back to the house on the beach.

We sat at the table, trying to wrap our heads around what had happened while Cash cooked something for us to eat. We were both still very much afraid that one of us would be next. We nibbled at our food in silence. The life that we knew was over, and this new life was going to be tough. The nagging question that kept circulating in my head was *How do I go on without my sisters?* They had been with me all of my life. They were always there to make sure their baby sister was okay.

On the way to take my niece home, we spent all the time reminiscing about how much fun we always had on our road trips to Georgia. The past was all we had, so we reveled in that. The future for the three of us had forever changed. We laughed about how my sister would always sit in the front passenger seat, but she never shared the driving. My niece and I did all the driving. We'd be driving down I-75, and we'd get behind a truck or an RV that was moving at a pretty decent speed, hoping to cut the drive time down. Those were the best of the times we had together.

On the ride back to the beach house, Cash quietly held my hand. He knew what I was thinking, and he knew how badly I was hurting. When we arrived back at the house, he showed me the photos he had taken while I spent those final moments with my sister. Even though I was angry and upset, that was the least of my worries. I never thought that God would let this sort of thing happen to me. Before this, I thought I was his child. I felt that he loved me. I was so full of faith. Now I just felt empty, lost, and alone.

I spent another few days with my family before I flew back to Atlanta. In just a few months, I'd be moving back home permanently; only home was now going to be missing a couple of people. I tried repeatedly, but I still could not find a Bible verse that would bring me comfort this time around. Don't get me wrong; it's not that I wanted to be ungrateful. I was just so overwhelmed by the pain of losing both of my sisters back-to-back; I couldn't think rationally or logically most of the time.

For months, I would go to work every day and feel the misery of not talking to my sisters the way I always had. After the first loss, I proclaimed how much trust and faith I still had in God. It would have been no problem to shout it from a rooftop if I needed to do that. But this time, I had so many questions.

Now God had gone and did it again—He took my last sister—what was I supposed to feel? What was I supposed to think? What plan did God have for this? Did He expect me to still shout from a rooftop? Who was I going to talk to now that both sisters were gone? So many questions, yet no answers.

With no comforting Scripture to keep my mind at peace, it seemed that I had put God on trial. I had to decide if I still trusted Him. Honestly, the jury was still out. I thought I knew what I believed. Now was the time for me to find out.

FOUND INNOCENT

If I thought living in Georgia with both my sisters gone was hard, it was much more challenging when I moved back home in June 2016. I stayed with a friend until I was able to find a more permanent place. My sister lived just south of the street that I would typically take when going home to the beach. Just one straight shot across the causeway, and I'd be home.

Before my sister passed, I would stop by her house sometimes on my way home. Afterward, every time I would be heading down I-95 toward that exit, I would get feelings of nausea. It wasn't long before I realized that I couldn't drive that way anymore. The memories were too painful, so I started taking a different exit on my route to home. It took longer that way, but I didn't mind as long as I avoided the memories.

I was faithfully attending church while I lived in Milton, Georgia, before my sister died. After she died, I stopped going to church for months. What was the point anyway? I thought. God was not there for me. So with the antics of a petulant child, I decided I was sitting this one out until God gave me the answers I felt I deserved. It was my way of acting out because I felt God had done me wrong, and I was going to show Him my displeasures. It was my humanity at odds with the divine Creator.

After months of wallowing in my despair, I thought, how would I ever win this fight with God when I couldn't even dry my tears? Slowly I started to remember what I had so easily forgotten. I had forgotten that were it not for God's amazing grace; there would be no me. But I was lost, you see. My ability to reason got swallowed up in my pain. My misery blinded me, and in my blindness, I only saw what I was feeling.

But I thank God for His mercies. Just as any earthly father would do, God, my heavenly Father, lovingly waited for me to come to myself. His chastisement was always His boundless mercy and unfailing love. So He waited, careful to never leave me alone, even when I chose not to acknowledge Him, even when I decided to think that He was not there for me. Indeed, there was a battle going on, but it was not a battle of God against me. It was a battle where God was fighting with me and for me. It was a battle that He, Jehovah-Nissi, would not lose!

It is said that the journey of a thousand miles begins with the first step. I decided then that my first steps would be to start reading my Bible again and go back to church. It did not matter if it was every now and then.

I CAN SEE CLEARLY

The year 2017 came in when I realized that months had passed filled with doubt and anger, but I was finally getting around to seeing things as they were. Like the prodigal son, only as the daughter, I arose and went to my Father. I needed to tell Him about my cares. God did not take my sisters from me, although I know that nothing happens to any of His creation unless He allows it and uses the situation to test His children.

Admittedly some tests are much harder than others. I heard someone say, the harder the test, the more God will reveal Himself to the one tested. Well, I thought, my tests were way too hard for me. Surely I had failed this one. I had failed to remember that every tear I shed, Jesus was right there, shedding those tears with me. I had failed to remember that every sleepless night that I was up, Jesus was up with me until I could fall asleep again. I had failed to remember that only Jesus could give me peace during this storm that had taken up an unwelcome residence in my spirit.

My heart just ached from the pain and regret of what would never be in this life. As time passed, I began to realize that God did indeed have a plan, even for this situation. Amid the pain, He brought back to my memory the last conversation I had with my sister. Even though she was pretty stressed out, we still enjoyed our time talking as we always did. For the first time in a long while, I was able to smile.

As I gradually eased my way back to attending church, the cobwebs began to make way for truth. I realized how God had lovingly given me that time with her that day. I was the last person to speak to her.

Thank heaven that the word of God had been planted in me from my youth even to this day. His words were rooted in my heart. Jesus promised that He would never leave us or forsake us. He promised us the comfort of His Holy Spirit in times of great distress. Quietly, in the background, the Holy Spirit was working in my heart and on my faith until I was ready to accept my loss.

The absolute truth is that the true enemy is still out there. It is the deceiver that was cast out of heaven. He is the known enemy of God and God's people. He has been here on this earth for thousands of years and has perfected the art of manipulating God's people. He is constantly sowing seeds of doubt, causing chaos, and defaming God's name. I had no intentions of being counted as one of those who sided with the enemy against God.

I wasn't exactly sure how I would move forward, but I knew that in regaining my faith once again, God would lead the way. Psalm 119:105 says "Thy word is a lamp unto my feet, and a light unto my path." Proverbs 3:6 says, "In all thy ways acknowledge Him, and He shall direct thy path." Once overshadowed in darkness, the light was now shining again. The Scriptures were coming back to me. With both my sisters gone, I was the only daughter my mother had left. I don't think she understood that, though, or at least I hoped she didn't. I was in enough pain for both of us. It was just the two of us left now, and we would make it together.

Come, Thou Fount of Every Blessing

Come, thou Fount of every blessing,
Tune my heart to sing thy grace;
Streams of mercy, never ceasing,
Call for songs of loudest praise.
Teach me some melodious sonnet,
Sung by flaming tongues above.
Praise the mount! I'm fixed upon it,
Mount of thy redeeming love.

Here I raise my Ebenezer,
Hither by thy help I've come;
And I hope, by thy good pleasure,
Safely to arrive at home.
Jesus sought me when a stranger
Wandering from the fold of God;
He to rescue me from danger,
Interposed his precious blood.

O to grace how great a debtor
Daily I'm constrained to be!
Let thy goodness, like a fetter,
Bind my wandering heart to thee.
Prone to wander, Lord, I feel it,
Prone to leave the God I love;
Here's my heart, Lord take and seal it
Seal it for thy courts above.

—Robert Robertson

Questions

My God, I fear I do not know the reason
why I'm here
I'm asking you on bended knees to somehow
make it clear
My eyes are blind, I cannot see, though, Lord,
you know I've tried
Have mercy on this wretched soul, your face,
Lord, do not hide
Please light my path and guide my feet, till all
I see is you
My morning star, my guiding light in everything
I do

—Valencia McMahon

ARE YOU SURE THERE IS A GOD?

I had been through my season of doubt and loss of faith. It wasn't pretty. I had never known how difficult life could be when you live it without faith, when you live it without hope, and when you live it in fear until adversities beset me. I came to realize that these human emotions are not foreign to God's people.

What I also came to realize is that God is faithful. He is that good shepherd who searches for even one lost sheep, though ninety-nine are safe at home. He is that loving father who would receive a wayward son or daughter back into the fold, no matter what they had done. He is that father who is full of infinite grace and mercy. He is full of infinite love and forgiveness. He is the God who parted the Red Sea to deliver His children out of Egyptian bondage. He is that bridge over the troubled waters in your life. He is the God who gave His only begotten Son to die for our sins. He is any and everything we allow Him to be when we walk in His ways.

One fact of life is that trials will come. Even Jesus had to endure the cross for our sakes. If ever there was anyone who could doubt whether there was a God, it was Jesus. For a brief period, Jesus became separated from His Father. That separation was due to the horror of the sins he bore for the world.

As any good father would do when his child is gone, God called for His Son to come home on the third day. And just as any good child would do, Jesus answered. It is because of that answer that we have hope, and we have a future.

With all of the bad things happening around and to us, it's only natural to wonder if there is a God. The answer to this question is seen in all of creation. It is felt in the very air that we breathe. And most importantly, the answer is found on the cross. Dare we think that it is by chance or by our power that we wake up each day? Not even our strongest enemy can give life. Yes, there is a God, and it is when we open our eyes to see His blessings all around us, we believe that this is so.

THE MATTIE KEMP STORY

A MOTHER'S LOVE

My mother had ten children, and she raised us all on her own. I don't know how she did it, but she did. I'm guessing it was only by the grace of God. For me, there was never a father as I grew up. My mother did remarry, so there was a kind of father figure while I was still young, though I did not consider him to be so. After he passed away, my mother did not remarry.

Despite not growing up with my biological father, I think I turned out pretty well. Proof that my heavenly Father was watching over me. I can still close my eyes and see my mom walking down the sidewalk with her kids heading to the church that we attended at that time. As I grew older, it ended up with just my mother and me attending church every Sabbath.

I can honestly say that I can attribute the character traits that I now possess back to my early childhood upbringing. My mother made sure I had the right foundation while in my youth. God had entrusted her, as with all parents, a very solemn task. I am living proof of Proverbs 22:6, "Train up a child in the way he should go: and when he is old, he will not depart from it."

During my teenage and early adult years, I may have tried doing a few of the worldly things like going to dances or listening to the latest pop music, but I was never inclined to smoke or drink or do any drugs. My foundation was solid when it came to those things. Once I grew into my thirties and older, I started to rely on my Christian upbringing more and more. I had my mother to thank for that. She had a tough job raising us, and from where I stand, she did her job.

We didn't always make the best decisions that would reflect the values she instilled in us, but that was on us.

My mom's philosophy was if you wanted something done, you had to do it yourself. She never learned to drive, so numerous times I remember seeing her getting on her bike and riding down to the store to get a few items to cook. Other times we would all be outside taking turns riding on her bike. I enjoyed watching her pedal her bike fast, then take her feet off the pedals then stretch both legs out and coast down the street. That memory always makes me smile.

My grandparents on my mother's side passed away long before I was born, so I never got the chance to know them. My oldest sister did, and she would often tell us that my mom got her cooking skills from her mother. I have to say, those were some mean cooking skills. We didn't have a fancy house or anything fancy for that matter, but we had what we needed.

She would always tell us God would provide, and He always did. We always had a roof over our heads, clothes on our backs, and food for our stomachs. Speaking of food, I can almost smell those Sunday morning breakfasts or dinners she would prepare. Some of my favorite foods were the northern or pinto beans with smoked turkey meat, rice, and those famous cornbread patties.

The Sunday morning breakfasts were the best, especially when she made her homemade biscuits. There was always chaos in the kitchen right after they came out of the oven. It seems she never made enough. Often she would take pity on us and make another pan. That was my mom. I remember how I used to hang around the kitchen just watching her work her magic kneading the dough, thinking, *I'm going to do that one day.*

When I moved into my place, I was determined to make homemade biscuits just as well as my mom did. It never happened, but I did manage to eat them after I baked them. I even had others eat them as well.

My mom had a heart of gold when it came to her children and her grandchildren. She loved us all. I remember how she used to play with us. She was so full of energy. When it came to discipline, she was good at that. You didn't want to get on her wrong side. Often her go-to weapon of choice was words. And not just any words either. She'd go lethal and start quoting the Bible. I think that was her way of making us feel guilty about our behavior. I'm happy to say that I was not on the receiving end of those words often. Nevertheless, she used them on me as well.

There were times when, for no reason at all, my mom would call each of us on the phone and start fussing. I can laugh now because whoever received the call first, that person would quickly reach out to the other sibling and say, "Mom is on the warpath." If she happened to call my sisters first, I made sure I didn't pick up the call. I played it smart and called the next day after she had calmed down. Looking back, I can say that those were memorable times with my mom. All filled with love.

IT'S MOM'S TURN NOW

As I look back now, I can see that I admired my mom, though it might have been hard to tell at times. Living on my own as an adult, I could see so much of her ways in me. I still can't go to bed at night and leave dishes in the sink. If my mom woke in the middle of the night and there were dishes in the sink, she would wake everyone up, no matter what time it was. It didn't matter whose turn it was to do them; we all had to get up until they were cleaned and put away. Those were the days.

When my mom was diagnosed with Alzheimer's, none of us understood the toll it would eventually take on her. After my oldest sister left her home to move in with my mom, she was still able to carry on as usual for a while. She was still able to have ordinary conversations or do many physical things with little or no assistance from anyone. I would go over to my mother's house on weekends, and it would be just the four girls—my mom, my sisters, and me. Even with only the four of us, we would still have a memorable time. I can still smile as I think back on those precious moments. Eventually, my mom could no longer get around without a wheelchair due to an injury she sustained years before. She was too stubborn to go for therapy, so the damage from the fall off her bike had never healed.

After moving to Alpharetta, Georgia, I would often call back home to talk to my sisters and my mom. Sometimes all of them would be together at my mom's place. Most times, my mom would say a few words to me, but we didn't have long conversations anymore. Sometimes when she wasn't able to speak, my sister would still put the phone to her ear so she could hear my voice on the other end. She always knew it was me because my sister would be saying in the background that she was smiling. Afterward, I'd speak to my sister again, say our goodbyes and I-love-yous, and then hang up. I always remember thinking it had been a long time since I had heard my mother's voice. I had not forgotten the sound of her voice. I just hadn't heard it in a very long time.

When I moved back home in 2016, one of my older brothers, who had retired, lived at the house with my mom. My sister never said it was an easy task, and anyone could see that. Now my older brother would experience what the day-to-day activities were like. He would be the one who would be responsible for her daily needs, including getting her to the doctor. The family would go over to visit, but somehow it just was not the same.

The atmosphere in the home had changed. For a bit longer, my mom was able to sit in her wheelchair and interact with others, if only through gestures. Eventually, she started spending all of her days in bed because she could no longer sit up in the wheelchair. When I would visit her, she'd be in her bed watching television, either a religious channel or one of the western movies she loved so much. Sometimes I would talk to her so she could hear my voice; other times, I'd just sit with her. She knew I was there. I had to take that knowledge as satisfaction since she could not speak the words.

By March 2017, my mother had become ill. When she didn't get better, she was taken to the hospital and later admitted. A couple of weeks later, her test results revealed that she had an infection that was causing the symptoms she was experiencing. I was working in Weston, Florida, at the time, which made it easy for me to drive to the hospital after work to visit with her. I can't tell you how much I wished my mother was able to communicate with us.

She would often try to tell us something, but because of her speech problem caused by Alzheimer's, it was difficult, if not impossible, to make out the words she was saying. Most of the time, I was the only one who could figure out what she was saying to us. I didn't think of it then, but what a blessing from God that I was able to tell the others what she was trying to say. I could see the relief on her face when I did so. I thought to myself, it would be a blessing to have a coherent conversation with her.

Even though the disease had progressed, my mom never forgot any of her children. She always recognized our faces when she saw us or heard our voices. I would always watch her when a new family member entered the room just to see who she'd remember when they entered.

Her eyes always lit up when any of her children would enter the room—proof that a mother never forgets her child, even when she can't speak. So I now know for sure that my mother, though she was not able to talk to any of us, knew full well who her daughters were when we laid them both to rest.

ONE LAST EFFORT

By the time Friday, March 31, 2017, rolled around, I felt exhausted from all the extra driving. Before I left work, I decided that instead of visiting my mom, I would go straight home, which was in the opposite direction, and then see her on Saturday at the nursing home where she had been admitted the night before. The funny thing is, as I was driving toward the expressway to go home, I decided at the last minute that I would visit my mom to make sure she was okay.

This would be the first time that she would not be living at home going forward. When I arrived, my niece Robin was already there. My mom was sitting up in the bed. She had a sort of blank stare on her face, but other than that, she seemed to be okay. As always, she recognized my voice. When dinnertime came around, I was able to get her to eat most of her food, saying, "Come on, Mom, open up— one more bite." She would open her mouth and take the food to eat. In between eating, we were able to get her to drink water. Her eating was very encouraging to us.

Content that things were going to be okay, we started planning what items we would bring back the next day to decorate her new room. After turning her on her other side and making sure she was ready for the evening, we did our kiss good night and then headed back home.

It was seven p.m. when we started to get ready to head home. I wanted to make sure to get back home before it became dark. I remember thinking while I was driving home how good it was to see my mom finally eat. I still thought it odd that she had a blank stare on her face, almost like her eyes were glazed over. I quickly let the thought pass because she was alert enough to understand everything I was saying to her, so I was okay with that. She did all that I asked her to. Kudos to Mom!

I was exhausted when I got home. Cash had come over, so I relayed the events of that day to him as we sat down for dinner. I went to bed that night happy I had seen my mom, and I was looking forward to getting up early the following day in order to be at the nursing home by seven a.m. to talk with one of the nurses in particular.

Sometime, in the middle of the night, I heard what I thought was the phone ringing. I wasn't sure if I was dreaming. It turned out that my phone was indeed ringing. I thought to myself, *The phone ringing in the middle of the night can't be good*, but I certainly didn't expect the news that I received. It was my niece. She had been the bearer of bad news before. She told me that in the middle of the night, my mom, her grandmother, had passed quietly in her sleep.

I just hung my head. *Here we go again. Where in the world did this come from?* I thought. "God, would You please just give me a break here, please?" I hadn't even recovered from losing both of my sisters, not to mention that Cash and I were dealing with some severe things concerning his health. He was fine at that time, but we still had gone through something pretty frightening.

I did not rest well for the remainder of that night. In the daylight hours, I met up with my brother, sister-in-law, and niece at the funeral home to plan my mother's funeral services. It was intense in there, but we got through it. The only thing left now was to bring in the items for her service. I was all too familiar with this process. I had been in this painful position before with my sister the previous year. Just like the last time, I hated every moment of it! Just as the times before, I needed much comforting.

FIGHTING FOR FAITH AGAIN

Though I hadn't quite gotten back to that firm foundation I had previously enjoyed with my faith in God, when my eldest sister died, I was much better than after my second sister who suddenly died. I longed for that faith and trust in God as I had before my eldest sister died. I desperately needed my soul healed. Was God there? Was He listening to me? Did He know I was hurting?

A myriad of questions flooded my mind, questions with no answers. At least no answers that made any sense to me at that time. I was leaning on Cash for his quiet strength. I felt as if I was aimlessly wandering alone in the valley of uncertainty. I needed to get back to my roots. So I continued to read the scriptures.

In the days leading up to my mother's funeral service, I took the time to wrestle with the thoughts that plagued my mind. Not only did things look really bad; they were really bad. As true as that was, I was not ready to give up on God. My mother would not be pleased. God would not be happy. I picked up my Bible, and I turned to my old favorite: "'He that dwelleth in the secret place of the most High shall abide under the shadow of the Almighty. I will say of the Lord, he is my refuge and my fortress: my God; in him will I trust" (Psalm 91:1–2). I started to remember the chorus to my mother's favorite song by James Cleveland.

> I don't feel no ways tired;
> I've come too far from where I started from.
> Nobody told me that the road would be easy;
> I don't believe He brought me this far to leave me.

It brought joy to my heart. She had endured a lot the last few years of her life. But I know she was glad she trusted in the God who created all things. She never got the chance to tell me if she still believed those words before she died. But I'm willing to bet she did still believe them.

At the service for my mom, I still watched her intensely, but I was not looking for her reactions this time. I saw a mother blessed with ninety-four years of life, though several of them had been difficult for her. I saw a mother who raised me and gave me a great foundation. I saw a mother who faithfully served her God. I saw a mother who shed many tears and bore the pain, shame, and disappointment from the consequences of many unwise decisions made by some of her children. I was looking at the mother, my mother, who was now on the edge and resting in Jesus. And so I decided then that God was indeed worthy of all the faith and trust I could muster. Though my faith was only the size of a mustard seed, I knew God could work with that.

After all, it was God who sent Jesus, His only begotten Son, to die for a world full of sinners. I was one of those sinners, I thought. There is a story in the Bible on belief found in Mark chapter 9, verses16–27. It tells of a man who sought Jesus in hopes that he would cast out the evil spirit in his son. Jesus, wanting to test the father's faith, said, "If thou canst believe, all things are possible to him that believeth." Then the father cried out immediately in verse 24 and said with tears, "Lord, I believe; help thou mine unbelief." The Bible tells us that instantly the man's son received healing.

That was it. It wasn't that I didn't believe; I needed help with my unbelief. That unbelief had existed because I had let doubt and fear creep into my mind and heart, causing a division within myself. The Bible tells us in Mark 3:25 that a house divided against itself cannot stand. Boy, don't I know that to be true. I felt as though I was standing on one foot, wobbling from side to side, trying not to fall. Soon I would be on solid ground again.

WHAT WAS EASY

There was nothing easy about losing my mom. There was nothing easy about laying her body to rest. What was easy, though, was knowing whom my mom put her trust in. What was easy was the gift that could only come from the all-knowing and loving God. God knew my mother would not be there for me on Saturday morning the way I thought she would be. It was He who impressed upon my heart through His Holy Spirit to go and see her on that Friday after work. I will never forget that time. It was a gift most precious.

In a short period, I had lost both sisters and now my mom. I had determined in my mind that Jesus is faithful to His word. Again I recalled the words that Jesus said in John 14:1–3:

> Let not your heart be troubled: ye believe in God, believe also in me. In my Father's house are many mansions. If it were not so, I would have told you. I go to prepare a place for you. And if I go and prepare a place for you, I will come again, and receive you unto myself; that where I am, there ye may be also.

There was going to be a resurrection, and I was going to see my mother and sisters again. I hope to see my bothers as well. The book of 1 Thessalonians 4:16 tells us that "the Lord himself shall descend from heaven with a shout … and the dead in Christ shall rise first." Ah, yes, that's easy to digest. I told myself if I focused only on death,

I would not find peace. If I could not find peace, then I would be making Jesus's promise void. Hope is what I now have. It's a hope that will carry me through until I see Jesus face to face. Mom is now resting.

Amazing Grace

Amazing grace! (How sweet the sound)
That saved a wretch like me.
I once was lost, but now I'm found,
Was blind, but now I see

'Twas grace that taught my heart to fear
And grace my fears relieved
How precious did that grace appear
The hour I first believed

The Lord hath promised good to me,
His word my hope secures;
He will my shield and portion be
As long as life endures.

Through many dangers, toils and snares
We have already come.
'Twas grace that brought us safe thus far
And grace will lead us home.

—John Newton

Great Hands

My dearest mother, you've gone away
From a world so marred by sin.
I lift my eyes and say: Thank you, Mom.
Great hands you've left me in.

The days are long, and the nights are cold.
The battle still rages within.
I lift my head and say: Thank you, Mom.
For great hands you've left me in.

These hands are not just any hands;
Their works are firm and true,
To shape, to mold, to gently guide
No mortal man can do.

These hands were pierced for the price of love;
The victory I will win
I lift my heart to thank you, Mom;
For great hands you've left me in.

—Valencia McMahon

IF THERE IS A GOD, WHERE DID HE GO?

Just when you think you have things figured out, wham! Life throws you another curveball that smacks you right upside the head. You feel the pain, but you don't know if you should be angry first at the situation that suddenly hit you or nurse the pain until it subsides. Either way, you know you're in for a rough ride. Like the rapid fire of a machine gun, I had lost both sisters and then my mother.

You could imagine the pain I was feeling. Even with all the pain, I still had the one person in my life that was my quiet strength. He was my rock. God had put him there, I'm sure, to be a blessing for me.

But the enemy of God's people was not ready to give up on me yet. This enemy figured he had one more trick up his sleeve, and he had prepared to play it on me. This trick was sure to be his best one yet. All I know is that the Bible says to resist the devil, and he will flee. As if anyone would want him around anyway. His job is to bring pain and chaos to make God's people miserable and separate them from God.

After my mother passed away, I believed that I would find some rest from the sting of death I had asked God to keep from me—at least for a long time. Behind the scenes, the great deceiver was gearing up to bring a great deal more pain my way. In the midst of our darkest nights, does God allow it? Does he say to the deceiver, "Have at it," and just disappear right when we need Him most?

I remember the poem "Footprints." Every time the writer finds himself going through the worst times in his life, he sees only one set of footprints in the sand. What he comes to realize later is that those footprints belong to Jesus. He is the one carrying the poet safely through the worst times in his life.

I can honestly say that on occasions, I have felt as if God had left me alone. If He had not left me alone, then I couldn't possibly be having these problems. What I needed to understand was that it was because I was never alone that I had these problems. There is a war going on, and God has engaged the enemy on our behalf. So if you feel He is missing in your darkest hour, open your spiritual eyes, and then look up. He is there in the light. We are never alone!

THE CASH MCMAHON STORY

THE GRIP OF DEATH

"Do you know what bank he used? Is your name on his bank account? Do you know how much money is in his account? He promised someone his car. He promised someone the television. Do you know where the lamps are?"

I vaguely remember these questions being thrown at me as I slowly came out of the daze. It was four p.m. on May 29, 2018, that I rested at my husband's bedside with my head on his chest, tears rolling down my face as I felt him breathe his last breath. I could not believe that it had all come down to this moment after all the prayers and silent requests. God had not answered our prayers and spared the life of the man that I loved with all my heart. My husband of six months was gone. The doctor had arrived at that moment only to check his heart and confirm that my husband was indeed no longer among the living. Cash McMahon was gone.

Ours was a long journey, with a unique set of ups and downs, yet our love was always strong. It saw us through all the good and not-so-good times. It eventually brought Cash and me together as husband and wife. I had just moved back home in June 2016 and was looking for a more permanent place for the future. I had already lost both my sisters, the oldest just before Christmas in December 2015 and the second a couple of weeks later, on January 2, 2016. I was more than happy to be back home with someone who was always there to support and comfort me. Cash and I had become much closer by then. We had started to talk about setting a date for our wedding again. Things were finally going our way.

It was the end of June, and we were both looking at houses to buy when he became very ill, so we went home. He felt no better that evening, so I took him to the nearby hospital's emergency room. After various tests and x-rays, they found something in the area of his stomach, which required further review, so he was admitted. The following day, the doctors had discovered a tumor in his stomach lining and advised that surgery was necessary to decide on the type and the severity of the tumor.

They scheduled the surgery for early evening on a Wednesday. I was at work that day but not able to concentrate. I counted down the time to when I could leave and join him at the hospital. We both just wanted the surgery to be over with so we could know what the problem was. As timing would have it, I was getting off the elevator on the floor of his room, just as the other elevator door opened, and there he was on the stretcher, being carried to his room. He looked at me, and we smiled at each other. I was so happy to see him. I reached out and held his hand, walking down the hall to his room.

When he got settled in, he told me the news. It wasn't good news, unfortunately. He had stomach cancer. Until then, I had never heard of stomach cancer. He told me the surgeon said he could not remove the tumor and that his entire stomach lining was like glue. The cancer had spread throughout the lining of his stomach. He had to stay in the hospital for a few days to recover from the surgery.

On Friday, July 1, the oncologist came into the room to check on him and discuss his treatment plan. As he was leaving, Cash asked him what stage his cancer was. It had been a couple of days since his surgery, and we still didn't know at what stage the cancer was. I'll never forget the words I heard next as the doctor turned to Cash and said, "Stage four." I was standing by the window looking out at Biscayne Bay. My body immediately froze. I was horrified because I had heard those ugly words before. Stage four was the last stage before certain death.

Still dealing with all the sleepless nights and the pain of losing my two sisters, I thought God would not put me through another loss so soon. Not this time. Not him. Especially since Cash and I had just recently gotten back together several months before. I thought about our wedding, and I remember thinking that I deserved to be happy with this man. Surely God would not take him from me now.

Instinctively I knew that God loved Cash and me, so I internally pleaded with God to allow me some happiness in my life. I remember saying, "God, please don't take him away from me too," as I looked out of the fifth-floor window before turning to him. I faked a smile that I'm sure did not quite reach my eyes and went to him. I was determined to remain strong for him.

You would probably expect the person who received such bad news to break down and cry or become hysterical, but he didn't. I know he must have been devastated on the inside, but he never let it show. Cash always had a quiet kind of strength, and it was on full display in that hospital room. I didn't know what to do or how things would turn out, but I knew I had to be as strong for him as he was for me. To win this battle of the mind, I needed to let my faith in God shine to carry us through this nightmare. If only I still had that level of faith.

He got discharged on July 3, 2016, and a few days later, he was to begin chemotherapy. While on chemotherapy, he discovered a special tea that was supposed to be excellent for fighting cancer. He started drinking the tea while having the chemo treatment. I knew it would take a miracle, and I had very little faith at that time that he would receive one. Still, I kept praying.

We saw very little change in the first couple of months. He was still not able to consume any solid foods, so he was surviving on chicken broth. His weight dropped to 133 pounds. He had become weak, and he could hardly get around by himself. I kept on praying, hoping that God would remember me and at least answer my prayers this time—especially since He had let my sister die not long ago. *God is good, isn't He?* I thought—a life saved for a life lost. I was still in the valley, questioning my faith. I had been there for months. Still, there was a small part of me hoping God would not let me down this time.

One day I was lying down in bed, totally beside myself. I just couldn't hold back the tears. To comfort me as he always did, Cash sat down in the chair next to me and began telling me how he had made peace with everything should he not survive cancer, as the doctors expected him not to. I just sat there in the bed, looking at him, trying to be strong for him. He told me that he would be okay as long as he knew that I would be okay and that his family would be okay. It was the first time he became emotional and cried. He cried because the new life we were looking forward to was now threatened. Cash laughed a little and said that one of the many side effects of the chemo was that it dried up the tear ducts, so even when he cried, the teardrops would not flow as they normally would have. But that did not make his sorrow any less. My tears were able to fall, and fall they did. The prayers continued.

By the third month, the treatments continued, and he was still drinking the tea and consuming chicken broth to give his body some kind of nutrition. One evening when I arrived home, he told me that earlier that day, he had heard this growling in his stomach that was much different than the growling, he was used to hearing. It was deafening, and he could see his stomach moving.

Shortly after that, he became hungry, so he decided to eat a softly cooked egg. After he had no ill effects from eating the egg, we figured if we could keep doing that every day, that would be a positive step forward. For weeks he ate softly cooked eggs. He still did not have his full strength back, but I knew we had to keep working at it. I wanted to believe that God was on our side. But I couldn't be sure just yet. We needed that miracle.

MIRACLE OR MADNESS

I started taking him on short walks at night to help build his strength. In the beginning, he was only able to walk maybe half a block before he became weak, so we would turn around and go back home. It was rough for a while, but he never gave up. He never got depressed. Within a few more weeks, he added more items to the softly cooked eggs to give him more calories for strength.

In doing this, gradually, he was able to put on more weight. The nighttime walks became longer until he was able to walk the distance that we used to walk many months before. We were beginning to see more of the light, and I wanted to have faith again, so I allowed myself a tiny bit of hope.

By the end of 2016, his doctor told him there was no trace of cancer. He was cancer-free. Could this be real? It was practically unheard of, and the doctors were all amazed. Everyone was surprised at the news. When he received the diagnosis, the doctors told him he barely had two weeks to live. At that moment, I thought, *To God be the glory*. I wanted to have faith in God again, and we needed that miracle—I needed that miracle. God gave it to us.

Not only had I read about some of the miracles in the Bible, but I had seen one as well. How blessed were we that God had bent His ear and answered our prayers! A life saved for the life of my sister that died. The miracle that we needed had certainly been performed, and I was now a witness. Friends and family alike were all amazed. I was happy to tell them about our very own miracle in 2016. A Christmas miracle was what we decided to call it. So much had happened over the past several months, but that trumped everything.

Within the first couple of months of 2017, the doctor changed his treatment to a reduced dosage in pill form. Again another major hurdle passed. We enjoyed months of his steady progress. Did I dare to even hope for our future again? It seemed that the future we talked about even before I moved back home was very much possible now. I began to hope again for our wedding—a wedding we both wanted for the immediate future.

By March, Cash was back working full force on the many projects he had put in motion years and months before. He was a kind and generous man who often was involved in charity auctions. He loved helping people when he could. While Cash was getting better, my mom was not. In the middle of the night, a call came in informing me that my mother had died. I was shocked because I had just seen her mere hours before. It was as if my entire life had taken on a crisis mode. People like to say that God will not give you more than you can handle. Well, I figured they have never been in my shoes. I thought, *God must think I can handle a lot,* because both my sisters were gone, my mom was now gone, and my fiancé, soon-to-be husband, was barely out of the woods with his own life.

After my mom's funeral, we agreed that life was just too short, so we set a date for the wedding. Cash thought that November 12, 2017, his birthday, would be the perfect day for the wedding. It was perfect, I thought. A wedding on his birthday, the day we first met. I chuckled to myself because I thought he would surely never forget our anniversary.

When he returned home after visiting his mother in May, he became ill that evening. The next day he still did not feel well either. He did not have much of an appetite, but we assumed that it must have been something he had eaten that was causing the problem. After a few days of not getting better, he called the doctor and went in to have a CT scan done. The results came back showing he had a blockage in his small intestine, possibly caused by the tumor, which they could not remove, or from the scarring of the initial surgery.

He began to experience some complications and was admitted into the hospital to remove the fluids built up in his stomach caused by the blockage. Prayers were still going up for his recovery. I still had the mindset to keep the faith and continue to trust in God. After a week in the hospital, he came home. I was thankful for that. My fuel tank of faith seemed like it wanted to move in the negative direction, but I held on. Cash held on.

It was late June, and as we had prayed and expected, he got better. We did not expect anything less from God. I didn't expect anything less from God. By that time, I had made my decision. I was going to trust God no matter what. We knew He would be faithful to us. After that, the doctor decided to put him back on the original chemo treatment. It wasn't ideal, but we were ok living with that.

HEAVEN OR HELL

By September 2017, Cash had gained back most of the weight he had lost months before. Those summer months leading up to the wedding were the best we'd had since his diagnosis. It was like I had a brand-new fiancé. We loved life and all that God had given us. Our future was looking bright. Even though we were engaged, he did not consider it official until he placed the engagement ring on my finger—that is, once I finally decided I would wear one. He was a determined man, so he and my niece decided to plan a surprise bridal party for me. It was October 29, 2017, when he took me for breakfast at the Breaker's Hotel on Palm Beach Island in West Palm Beach, Florida. I asked him why we were going to such an expensive hotel just for breakfast. He just smiled and said, "I wanted to do something special with you today." He remembered that I once mentioned to him that I wanted to go there one day.

Upon arrival, we explored the hotel and the beautiful courtyard before making our way out to the beach. It was a windy day, and the sky was overcast. It felt like home. It had been a while since we heard the sound of the crashing waves in the ocean. As we looked out over the water, he began to tell me about all the things he had in his life and the joy that they had brought to him. When we sat down on the bench, he continued his story, and I listened intently. Cash was so happy. He reminded me of a kid in a candy store. As he was telling his story, a group of people walked by. I only noticed because a man was pushing a lady in a wheelchair.

When I looked back at Cash, I heard him say there was only one more thing that he needed in his life that would bring him fulfillment, and that one thing was me. I looked at him and smiled, then began to speak, but before I could get the words out, I noticed this small box that housed a beautiful diamond engagement ring when opened. I heard him ask again, "Will you marry me?"

I pretended to think about it for a moment and then laughed, as he looked at me with that you've got to be kidding me expression on his face. Naturally I said yes again, and seconds after my yes answer, that same group of people passed back by smiling and said congratulations. It dawned on me then that they could tell what was going to happen before I did. We had breakfast then headed back home a few hours later. Of course, when I saw all the cars at the house, I knew for sure something was going on.

TWO STEPS FORWARD, ONE STEP BACK

During the months leading up to the wedding, Cash had a couple of treatments and experienced some adverse reactions to the chemo treatments and advised the doctor about them. The reactions were severe enough to warrant no further treatment of the current medication. Thank God, both times he recovered. We were looking forward to getting married.

By November 11, 2017, all of the wedding party had arrived at the house. I remember thinking to myself how good God was. We were blessed, and we were about to accomplish our dream together. I knew God was answering another one of my prayers. The man that I was marrying was quite different from the man I met ten years earlier. I was different.

I allowed my mind to travel back to that special day of November 12, 2007, when we first met as strangers on a blind date. He was sitting at a table at an outside café. When I approached, he smiled, stood up, and pulled out a chair for me. Inwardly, I smiled as we sat there and talked. When we left to go for dinner, he had casually mentioned that that day was his birthday.

At first I thought he was kidding, but he assured me that it was true. I always thought that people deserved a hug on their birthday, and since that day was his birthday, he needed his hug. To Cash's surprise, I smiled and embraced him as I said, "Happy birthday." It was instant. By the time the embrace was over, something inside me had assured me that I would marry him one day. All I had to do was wait to see if my intuition would prove true.

MATCH MADE IN HEAVEN

November 12, 2017, had finally arrived, and I was the happiest woman in the world. Even better, my future husband was feeling excellent. We were getting married on his birthday. What could be better? I was marrying my best friend, who just happened to be the man that I loved dearly. I had known this day would come when I met him on this date ten years earlier. It felt like the face of God was finally smiling at us. There was no raining on this parade. Not on this beautiful day.

As I walked down the aisle, he looked so handsome standing at the altar in his tuxedo, smiling at me. I recognized that look in his eyes. He stood there, tall and proud. He was waiting for me, his bride adorned in angel wings to meet him there. It was a fairy tale wedding just as we had envisioned, with our very own little angels. Indeed a match made in heaven, we thought. I had prayed for this day for a long time. Now God had answered. Of course, we celebrated with family and friends. Before the evening was over, my new husband had made his way into the hearts of everyone. Our future never looked so bright, and we had God to thank for it all. That mustard seed of faith was turning into a tree firmly planted by the rivers of flowing water.

On Wednesday, November 15, 2017, I went back to work as Mrs. McMahon. He spent the last few hours with his best friend, who had stood as best man, before he went in for another chemo treatment. On my way home from work that day, a call came in from him. I could barely understand what he was saying, but I heard the pain in his voice. He told me he was at the hospital. Terrified, I asked, "What's wrong?" I couldn't tell if he said he was in the emergency room or not when the call dropped. I called right back, but there was no answer. I called the hospital, still concerned, and found that he was receiving treatment in the emergency room.

Dear God, please let my husband be okay. I kept repeating, *Please don't take him away from me.* My mother was gone, my two sisters were gone, so he was the only person that God put in my life that gave me the strength to keep it together. He was the only person who gave me the strength to carry on. *Please, God; don't take him away from me too.*

By the time I had arrived at the hospital, he was lying quietly on the bed in the hallway. They had given him something for the pain. Later he was admitted. When he awoke and was able to speak, he told me that he had been given the very same chemo treatment that had caused his two previous severe reactions. This time it was more painful than before. He explained that his entire insides felt severely damaged because of it. While he was in the hospital this time, they had to perform another procedure that would help remove some of the fluid buildup in his stomach. After several days in the hospital, he was able to come home. It was not the way either of us was thinking our honeymoon would be. He was a trouper, though.

The devil was at it again. He needed to stir up the waters and bring hell to our heaven on earth. He needed to give us both a reason to doubt God. His goal was to get us so fed up and angry with God for misleading us that we would turn from Him. The incredible thing was that even then, my husband showed no fear on his face or in his actions. He showed a determination that nothing was going to get him down. It was that quiet strength again. He was a man of positive thinking, and I loved him so much. I didn't know if he was drawing on the power of God or if he was strong for me. Whatever it was, he always seemed to have it.

By Thanksgiving, he was feeling fine, and we spent that holiday with his family. He didn't have another treatment until December 31,

2017. This time, he started with a new treatment that was supposed to be promising for people with his particular kind of condition. We did as many of the things he loved as we could. God blessed us, and we saw 2018 come in.

TRIAL BY FIRE

It's funny how things work out in life. On any given day, millions of people are facing all kinds of adversity. Out of the kindness of our hearts, we tend to offer what little support or advice we're able to give to those people. Most of the time, it can be ineffective because, for the most part, people don't know what to say. We find ourselves repeating the same old clichés we've heard from our parents, friends, and acquaintances. "God is good," we say; "everything happens for a reason." Perhaps the most repeated one is "God won't give us more than we can handle." I've often wondered whether we really believe those words when we say them, or are we merely trying to make other people feel better? I think that it's more of the latter.

Now don't misunderstand me. There's nothing wrong with those words of reassurance and encouragement. I believe that those words have more meaning when spoken with an experienced heart. When adversity knocks at your door, do you answer or just run and hide? If you answer, what do you say? If you run, where will you hide? Our relationship with God will determine our actions.

By February 2018, adversity was staring us down again. We were looking down the barrel of what felt like a loaded gun. Cash started to have problems with his stomach and once again was not able to consume food. We had done another CT scan, which now showed that the tumor had increased in size. The doctors did not have an answer, so they decided to throw radiation therapy in the mix. All that did was make my husband feel worse and become weaker.

By the end of February, my husband was back in the hospital. The only option left besides not doing anything was surgery to remove the damaged part of his intestines caused by the adverse reaction of the chemo treatment. The surgeon had three options he could do, depending on what he found once he went in. Options A and B were the preferred options, while option C was the "if all else fails" option. Here comes that old devil again. Option C was all the surgeon could do. My husband was in the hospital for six and a half weeks during recovery and rehabilitation. Everything seemed to be starting to go in the right direction again, from what we could see. He was back to walking and eating, so we came home on April 19, 2018.

Before this last ordeal, which landed him in the hospital, we had learned of an organization called Debbie's Dream Foundation. Their sole purpose was to educate the public and raise awareness and funding for stomach cancer research. Excited about what they were doing, Cash decided to get involved in what they were doing to help raise money in any way he could.

Within a few days, he had made contact, and the next thing I knew, he had volunteered to do a collage on the founder of that organization. The revealing of the collage would take place at their upcoming anniversary celebration. When my husband agreed to do the collage, he had no way of knowing when he made that commitment in 2017 that he would be in the hospital recovering from a life-threatening disease. To him, a promise made is a promise kept. He was not going to let his battle with stomach cancer get the best of him. He had no intentions of not honoring his word.

On April 15, 2018, he had me bring down all the supplies needed for the collage, including all the items he had received from the foundation to the rehabilitation center at the hospital. He was barely able to walk just yet, but with a determination that would make anyone take notice, he made his way down to the recreation room. In my peripheral view, I noticed some of the nurses watching him in amazement.

With the skills he had learned over the years, he masterfully laid out the piece the way he had already envisioned in his mind. He had an excellent eye for art. I never saw a beautiful flower that he did not stop and take a picture of. He said he would make art with them one day. It was he who pushed me to be the artist that I am today. Within a few days, the piece was completed. The nursing staff commented on how well he had done. I saw the smile on his face and the satisfaction in his eyes. He'd done it. He had not let his circumstances defeat him. Now the only thing left was to deliver it before the anniversary celebration a few days away.

I was happy to be taking him home on April 19 to continue his care until he was back on his feet again. We were heading straight home when I heard him say he wanted to drop off the piece at the foundation. I was a little stunned, I have to admit, but quickly assured him that I would deliver the work for him once I got him home resting. He replied, "No, honey, I want to deliver it. Please take me there." Within the hour, we were pulling into the parking lot of the foundation.

This walk was going to be much longer than the walk he did in the rehab center. I asked him, "Are you sure you're going to be able to walk that far?" With steely determination in his eyes, he just looked at me and said yes. This time, though, he lovingly allowed me to assist him. Once inside the foundation, he could sit for a bit before he met with some of the event coordinators. They loved the piece, and they were sure Debbie's family would love it as well. I saw his face relax a little, and I knew he was satisfied. He had kept his word. That meant a lot to him, I could tell.

Once I got him home resting, I was finally able to relax next to him. We had made it home with no incidents. I had so much admiration for this man who was now my husband. God had given him so much strength, and he always let it show. Shortly after the event was over, he received an email from the foundation regarding the article on the anniversary event. The article talked about him and the collage. He was pretty happy about that, and I was pleased with him.

For the first three weeks, things went well. Then an infection set in. We got it treated. After that, it seemed that nothing would work. He had problems every day that we did not expect. The doctor tried all kinds of medication in an effort to alleviate the symptoms. Nothing worked. On Friday, May 18, 2018, he had another CT scan done. All I could think was *God, if You hear me, don't let the news be bad news.*

BURNED BUT NOT CONSUMED

On Monday, May 21, 2018, we went to the doctor for the results and listened to something that I don't believe either one of us thought we would hear. The doctor told us that there was nothing else he could do. The new treatment was not working. I stood there just stunned, not knowing what to say.

Cash looked at him and asked him two questions. The first question was "How long do I have?" The second was "Why did you give me that last chemo treatment when you knew the adverse effect it had on me before? You told me you would not do that. Why, doctor, would you do that and not tell me? If you had told me you were going to give me the same treatment, I would have refused it."

I saw the raw disappointment on my husband's face, and I wanted to hold him right then and just cry. I know that old devil must have been grinning from ear to ear. I can imagine him saying with a look of victory in his eyes, "I got them. Where is their God now?" With nothing left to do, we went home to enjoy the time we had left together.

Cash was a joy to watch. He never complained. We still tried to have as normal a life as possible given our circumstances. On Tuesday, May 22, 2018, the pastor and first elder of my old church came over and prayed with us. By Thursday of that week, May 24, we were at the emergency room again. A few hours later, Cash got admitted to the hospital, but this time to the critical care unit. The oncologist had said he had a couple of months to live, so I wondered why that unit but figured it was because he needed a nurse more often.

It still had not dawned on us what was happening. At least it had not dawned on me yet. We did not understand the significance of Cash being in the critical care unit until the nurse explained a few things to us. It shocked us both. Again we remembered the oncologist's prognosis, and we were not expecting to hear anything different. Again we were facing those defining moments. We were facing another life-or-death situation. For sure, all things were pointing to certain death very soon. He did not have months to live.

Instead of the feeling of looking down the barrel of a loaded gun, it now felt as if we were in a boxing ring, and that old devil must have been dancing around the ring like Muhammad Ali, about to deliver his knockout punch. My husband only had days, maybe hours, to live. I called his mother and told her she needed to come. A new friend from my job came by to give me support. I stayed up all night Thursday watching him. I could not imagine losing him even though it was just a matter of time.

On Friday, May 25, 2018, after the doctors left with no good news, I could not hold back the tears. I did not want my husband to see me cry, but there was no way I could hold them back any longer. My mind could not imagine living without him. I felt the gentle caress of his hand running through my hair as I lay there facedown on his bed, crippled with pain, tears streaming down my face. He was offering me comfort, showing me his quiet strength.

When I looked up at him, he smiled at me, letting me know that he was okay with what was happening. I loved him even more for that. In my heart, I just asked God to give me the strength to bear this. He decided that he wanted to spend whatever time we had left together at home. That Friday night, he came back home where he belonged.

The next couple of days were average in that he was interacting with others as if he would be around for some time to come. We watched our wedding video one more time. Again I watched him smile. In between everything going on around us, I managed to sleep next to him all night on Saturday, May 26, 2018, with my arms wrapped securely around him as we slept. I was holding on to every last minute I could get with him.

Naturally, we said our I-love-yous as we had done so many times before. What precious time God was giving us. It was God's final gift of love to us in this life. The last thing my husband said to me when I asked what he wanted me to do concerning his business was "I trust you," and again he smiled at me. That was on Sunday, May 27, 2018. Monday went by way too quickly. It seemed like a blur, but I remember it all so well.

On Tuesday, May 29, I was beside my husband with my head gently resting on his chest, tears rolling down my cheeks, as he breathed his last breath at 4:00 p.m. The fight was over. The devil had pulled his arm back as far as he could and delivered the knockout punch. I vaguely remember whispering in my husband's ear that everything was going to be all right before the punch came. He had made his peace with God before he took his last breath, and I find great comfort in knowing that. I also find great comfort in knowing that my husband is now resting in Jesus, waiting on the resurrection to eternal life that He promised to all those who love and obey Him.

SAFE IN HIS ARMS

This time, not only had I lost my husband, I had also lost my best friend. I'd lost the man who for ten and a half years had been by my side. He was there giving me all of his quiet strength—giving me all of his support in my endeavors. I had lost the man who had stood beside me through all of my ups and downs. He was there when I lost my first sibling. He was there when I lost both of my sisters. He was there when I lost my mother. He was always there for me. The man who loved me unconditionally was gone.

I remember thinking of the vows that we made on our wedding day. I can still hear his voice as he spoke the words to me. He felt so blessed that he was able to fulfill his dream of marrying a beautiful and loving woman. We both were looking forward to a life full of blessings from above. He would always say his life was full of abundance, and it was. It was a short life in my eyes, but I always knew he enjoyed his life. The life we thought we would have together as husband and wife was not to be. That man would no longer be able to stand by my side to offer me his quiet strength.

That knockout punch from the devil not only took my husband's life; it also sent me tumbling off a mountain. Not because I did not have faith, but because it took me by surprise. That's what the devil does—take us by surprise. As I tumbled off that mountain, I was in desperate need of rescue. I needed far more than Psalm 91:11–12: "He shall give his angels charge over thee, to keep thee in all thy ways. They shall bear thee up in their hands, lest thou dash thy foot against a stone." This rescue called for someone who had the power to stop

Satan at what looked to be his finest moment. It called for someone who had stopped Satan before. I got struck hard, and I felt the pain from the sting of his blow for sure. I was down but not down for the count. And certainly not out. Jesus Himself, the creator of heaven and earth, the Savior of the world, lover of my soul, stepped in as I tumbled off that mountain. I could hear His voice like the sweet sound of music to my ears, saying, "I've got you, Valencia," as I fell safe into His loving arms. Psalm 91:2, 4 says, "I will say of the Lord, He is my refuge and my fortress: my God; in him will I trust .... He shall cover thee with his feathers, and under his wings shalt thou trust."

Now I don't know why God allowed my husband's death, especially when things began to look up. I don't even know what good will come out of this tragedy. I only know that something good will come out of it. God's reputation is on the line here. If all things truly work together for good, then something good will come out of this. For now, only the grace of God will get me through the rest of my life without my husband. After my first sister passed, I had declared that I still trusted God and had faith in Him. The days, weeks, months, and years ahead would determine if my words were merely that—words.

VALENCIA'S TESTIMONY

DEFINING MOMENT

For the next several days leading up to Cash's memorial service, I had absolutely no idea of what to do. It felt like the better part of me was gone. What would I do now? Many questions were going on in my head. In my heart, I knew that God was there, giving me the strength to get through one day at a time.

I cried many tears—Lord knows I did. I felt helpless but not hopeless at the same time. God's presence was with me. After my husband's service, when everyone had gone back to their lives, the weight of the knowledge that I would never come through the doors of our home and hear my husband welcome me home again hit me like the proverbial ton of bricks. I cried and cried and cried. Just when I thought I had no more tears, more tears came. I knew that there will be many more days to come filled with more tears.

I needed to find relief. I desperately searched through the halls of my mind recalling our conversations, our laughter, and all the times we spent together. Making sure the sound of his voice is indelibly imprinted there forever.

I didn't want to forget his voice. My soul, the very essence of my being, needed comforting! Family and friends had done what they could do for me. There was no denying that I was far beyond what they could do for me with their words. I needed the Comforter of all comforters. I needed Jesus to step in and guide me through this journey. I knew it would be difficult at best, simply because without my husband, I was alone. At least that's how I felt.

Yes, I've heard, as I said before, that God would not give me more than I can handle. But my reality was, at least in my mind, that God had indeed given me way more than I could handle in such a short time. Four of the most influential people in my life were gone. What was I to do now? They were the most significant part of my life. I've had people come to me and quote a part of Romans 8:28: "All things work together for good," etc. Of course, I had no reason to doubt that except that I struggled to see the good in any of my losses.

My husband once rhetorically asked the question, "Is this it? Are we simply born to live and then die? Is there nothing else?" Of course, he believed in God, and he knew that heaven was where he wanted to end up. It was just that life, when you take a look at it, is not what it's cracked up to be without God in it. We're here for a season, and then we're gone. Like vapors in the wind. Still, what was I going to do without my support? Will the real Valencia please stand up for the world to see?

I remember talking to my husband before he passed about how we would go to my church and tell everyone about his miracle in 2016.

Not that we hadn't been telling others all along. After we got married, I was sure that we were finally going to be able to do that. By the grace of God, I had the privilege of seeing my husband become the man I saw him to be some ten years earlier when we first met. He was in no way an undesirable person when I met him. I just knew he would become a better person spiritually.

Through the years, he had watched me. He saw me going to church, so he started going to church a little more. We began praying together. I heard my husband's prayers became more focused and specific. One of my greatest joys with him was when he accompanied me to church a couple of weeks after our marriage. When the call for special prayer came, I left my seat and went to the altar for prayer, leaving him in his seat. When I turned to the side, I could see that he was standing in the row behind me. An old family friend had gone to him, taken his hand, and walked to the altar with him. Bless her heart; I had brought him to church, and she had brought him to the altar before God. To see that he enjoyed himself that day brought even more joy to my heart.

I had come full circle. Now that the four most influential people in my life were gone, could I still declare that my faith in God was firm? The losses were so close together. After I lost my second sister, I did doubt for a while that God was there. I wasn't so sure I had any faith left. I started to wonder if I was one of those who simply spoke bold words, but when it came time to put those words to the test, would I fail miserably? God was watching, and time would tell.

When I lost my mother in 2017, I was back on the right track with my thinking. I was on the right track because I was back to reading the Bible more and learning how to trust God again. I knew He was with me because I felt His Holy Spirit gently guiding me until I could boldly make my declaration again. And so I can declare that I trust Him, and I had complete faith in Him even in my disappointment.

The most significant test, I believe, was the loss of my husband during the first six months of our marriage. I had to either walk the talk or stop lying to myself and telling others how good God is. There would be no half-stepping. God does not want followers who would only declare His goodness when times are good because He did not promise all good times. In fact, He tells us in John 16:33 that in this world, His followers will have tribulations, but we are to be of good cheer because He has overcome the world. Paul says in James 1:2–3 that we should count it all joy when we're beset with trials and tribulations. I know I have yet to attain that mindset of counting all my tribulations as joy, but I will continue to press toward that mark.

So even in the face of our greatest losses and disappointments, God's faithful followers will continue to declare His goodness. Often when people hear me talk about the four tragedies that forever changed my life, they respond with words like "You're so strong." I smile inside because I am not strong. There is nothing inside me that is even remotely strong. But I believe in a God who is strong. I believe in a God who can lift me up every minute that I am down. It is His strength alone that radiates inside and sustains me. I see His sovereign hand in all that has happened and is happening in my life. He is the faithful and true God. So with all that has happened, I either trust God or I don't. If I do, then the testimony that I prayed my husband would give was now mine to give in his stead. And so I declare to you, dear reader, that God is good, and yes, I trust Him.

TRIALS OF LOVE

Is God good? I've often heard people say, if there is a God and if He is so good, why does He allow bad things to happen to good people? There is much to say to that, but first, let me say, God doesn't just allow bad things to only happen to "good people." Bad things happen to all people. The Bible tells us that the sun shines on the just and the unjust.

Second, I would ask by whose standards are we measuring good? Matthew 19:17, Mark 10:18, and Luke 18:19 all tell us when the young ruler referred to Jesus as "good master," Jesus responded that "there is none good but one, that is, God." That same Bible tells us in Romans 3:23 that "all have sinned and come short of the glory of God." Romans 6:23 goes on to say, "The wages of sin is death, but the gift of God is eternal life." So if you believe the words of Jesus, then you know that in truth there are no "good people."

Allow me, however, to tell you about God, who clothed Himself in the frailty of humanity. He who did no wrong was abandoned, beaten, cursed, denied, spat upon, scorned, laughed at, and had a crown of thorns placed on His head; He was mocked and nailed to a cross. He died and rose the third day. He underwent all this so that He could redeem the so-called "good people," restoring the unity between God and man once and for all. No, my friend, there are no "good people." There are merely people who have chosen to accept Jesus as their Savior. It is His blood alone that makes us all worthy in God's eyes.

To fully understand the complexity of the question, "If God is good, why does he allow bad things to happen to good people?" you must first accept the sovereignty of God. Colossians 1:16 says that it is by His power and at His will that all things are created. They were created by Him and for Him. And when He chooses, He alone allows certain things to happen or not to happen. We must recognize that there are forces in this world that are warring against God and His people.

> For we wrestle not against flesh and blood, but against principalities, against powers, against the rulers of the darkness of this world, against spiritual wickedness in high. (Ephesians 6:12)

God simply cannot do bad things. He does not promote bad things. But He can certainly bring good results out of those bad things. So who is responsible for those bad things, you ask? Hear the words that Jesus told in His parable of the sower, found in Matthew 13:28: "An enemy has done this," He stated. An enemy indeed has done this. The same enemy who was cast out of heaven, the one that usurped Adam's authority has wreaked havoc on this world. From the day iniquity was found in him, he knew nothing but destruction (Ezekiel 28:14–15).

Still, being creatures of habit, we are prone to question God with a why when we don't understand when things happen. It seems that in our humanity, we tend to believe that we can cope better with adversity when we know the reason for the trouble. Somehow, knowing helps us manage, or so we tell ourselves.

I am undoubtedly guilty of asking God why. I think knowing why is significantly more important to us when we lose a loved one—especially when we pray for divine intervention, and there is none. I wanted desperately to know why I lost four of the most important people in my life. But I knew that if I chose to dwell on that line of thinking, I might have been led down a path of mistrust in God that could ultimately lead to self-destruction. That is what the enemy of God wants, and I had no plans to give him that victory.

With total deliberation, I shifted my thoughts and started asking myself why I was still here. That changed my focus. In my brokenness, I was able to see God's goodness and mercy. So it is not that God does not hear our prayers or that He doesn't answer our prayers. He is behind the scene working all things together for the good of all those who love Him.

The next time you find yourself praying and you feel that all you are hearing is the deafening sound of silence, I invite you to take a look at Jesus in the garden of Gethsemane. Take a look at Jesus on the cross. In the garden of Gethsemane, Jesus knew that His death was fast approaching, so He went to pray. Three times He asked His Father to take that cup of death from Him if it was at all possible for His Father to do so. He was in agony over the impending events and was desperately asking His Father if there was another way to save humanity other than the way of the cross.

Jesus did not want to die on the cross. He did not want to endure the unbearable pain of it all. Could you blame Him? Who would want to die for a fallen world that did not love them back? Three times Jesus pleaded with His Father, and each time, He said, "Nevertheless, thy will be done." Surely one would think that if anyone could get a response from God at such a trying time, it would be Jesus. Jesus was His only begotten Son.

What about the cross? I'm reminded of the words in Matthew 27:46, while hanging there on the cross, Jesus cried out, "My God, my God, why hast thou forsaken me?" There He was, hanging on a cross, suspended between heaven and earth, yet He received no response from His Father.

We must know that it was not that God could not have answered, nor that He could not have come down and taken His Son off that cross or prevented the whole thing in the beginning. No, God had to be God. He saw the entire picture—the greater good, if you will. For God to save humanity and reconcile us to Himself, Jesus, His only begotten Son, had to suffer, bleed, and die. God had to be silent. Can you think of a time when silence ever sounded so beautiful? Only a sovereign God with an unfathomable love for His creation could sit back and be silent while His plan of redemption unfolded. It was a redemptive plan that took the life of His Son.

The next time someone quotes Romans 8:28—"And we know that things work together for good to them that love God, to them who are the called according to His purpose"—consider what the Bible says in verse 32 of that same chapter: "He that spared not his own Son, but delivered Him up for us all, how shall He not with Him freely give us all things?" So in those silent moments when we don't get an answer, and we think that God does not hear us, remember, He gave up His only Son for all of humanity.

Our prayers get answered long before we prayed any of them. If we choose Him, in the end, we will see how all things do work together for good. So the real question should never be "Why does God allow bad things to happen to 'good people,'" but rather, "When God allows the bad things to happen to 'good people,' where do we, the 'good people,' stand? Do we continue to stand firm in our faith, trusting God completely? Or do we take the advice of Job's wife and simply curse God and die?" Remember God's words in Jeremiah 29:11 (NIV): "For I know the plans I have for you, declares the Lord, plans to prosper you and not to harm you, plans to give you hope and a future." If you do, your journey toward the kingdom of heaven will be sweet.

When my husband passed away, my oldest brother called, who had previously sworn off his family a long time ago. He was the brother who had said nothing to his family at our sister's and our mother's funerals—that same brother who did not even attend the funeral service of our middle sister. He was now sending his condolences. He was not able to attend my husband's memorial service, but he did send his wife. Now I'm not saying in any way that speaking to my brother again was worth the loss of my husband; I'm simply saying that good things do come out of bad situations, even when they are small things.

But we must know that more extraordinary things are yet to come. Recall the story of Joseph in the book of Genesis. He was the youngest and the most highly favored of his brothers by his father,

Jacob. Because of their jealousy, they plotted to kill him but instead sold him into slavery. For years his father mourned him, thinking Joseph was dead. Now here is where you see God's omniscience and divine providence at work. He knew years before that there would be a famine in the land, including Egypt, so He put Joseph there through slavery.

I believe that God never exalts anyone before that person has been humbled. By the time the famine hit, Joseph was second in command of all of Egypt. When his brothers came to Egypt for food, Joseph recognized them. Later, when he revealed himself to them, they became fearful. Seeing this, he said in Genesis 45:5–7, "Now therefore be not grieved, nor angry with yourselves, that ye sold me hither: for God did send me before you to preserve life …. And God sent me before you to preserve you a posterity in the earth, and to save your lives by a great deliverance."

What Joseph's brothers had meant for evil, God had meant for his good. In our pain, we must learn to recognize the hand of God working not only in our lives but the lives of those around us. If God had not put Joseph in Egypt, then there would not have been anyone there to interpret Pharaoh's dream; the famine would have still hit, and with no food preserved over the years, many would have perished. I never thought I would hear my brother apologize for anything, but he did, and all is well, regardless of his future actions.

GOOD FROM BAD

"My plans are to give you a hope and a future," God tells us. His plans are never to hurt us. So we must purpose in our hearts and believe that God has something far better in store for us. He alone fully understands the pain of loss. Can you imagine how God must have felt when Adam and Eve sinned? Imagine how God must have felt when He pronounced the death sentence on His creation. He did not create us to die.

Even in death, though, we must be willing to see and accept the sovereignty of God. Even in death, the glory of God will still be revealed. So if He does not stop a bad thing from happening, like losing a loved one, if we open our eyes and look closely, we will see how He will use it for His purpose. Can't fathom such a thing? Neither could I. God tells us in Isaiah 55:8–9 that His thoughts are not our thoughts, and His ways are not our ways. As the heavens are higher than the earth, so are His ways and thoughts higher than ours.

Lazarus' resurrection is one of the most memorable stories in the Bible about something good happening after something terrible. Remember, when Jesus got the news that Lazarus was sick, He purposely stayed where He was, only arriving four days after Lazarus had died. Though He knew the glory of God would be revealed, He still wept with Mary and Martha. He wept with them because He was able to sympathize with their human emotions. Mary and Martha were right: if Jesus had been there, Lazarus would not have died. After thanking God, Jesus said, "Lazarus, come forth." Lazarus came forth still bound. The Bible tells us that many of the Jews who saw that miracle believed. Now, if Lazarus had not died, there would not have been a resurrection. Do you see it? No death means no resurrection, and the people would not have believed in God. This story shows how we get something better than good from something bad. This resurrection is but a shadow of the resurrection to come. That is the resurrection I am looking forward to seeing my loved ones in.

Now I have to admit that sometimes God will do some unthinkable things to save us. Not out of desperation, but always out of love. God is love, so there is no other way that He would respond to His people.

> Behold what manner of love the Father hath bestowed upon us, that we should be called the sons of God. (1 John 3:1)

One of those unthinkable things is letting some die to save many more. I believe God did when it came to my husband. That is not to say that He did not love my husband, because He did. He died knowing that he had made his peace with God and had accepted Jesus.

I am so thankful that when my husband died, he did so while he was married to me, the woman he truly loved. In 2016 the doctors had said he would not survive the year, but God said otherwise. Our union was a gift most precious from God. And though my heart is saddened, my spirit sometimes weary, I know I will see him again. So now I give you this hope, this blessed assurance that God has given to me. Never fear evil things. Just know God's got it.

The group Mercy Me sings a song whose chorus goes like this: "I know you're able, and I know you can save through the fire with your mighty hand, but even if you don't, my hope is in you alone." Charles Wesley said it best in these words: "Father, I stretch my hands to thee, no other help I know; If Thou withdraw Thyself from me, oh whither shall I go?" So even if you don't believe in God, wouldn't bad things still happen anyway? Of course, they would. Only with God, you know that if or when He chooses, His children will be spared some of the bad things, knowing full well that their reward is coming. "Choose you this day whom you will serve; as for me, I will serve the Lord." By now, you must know that life won't always be a bed of roses. I know this for sure because I've had plenty of thorns in my flesh. And some of those thorns still linger.

ONE ON ONE

Knowing full well that we won't always have roses, how do we survive the crises? It is our relationship with God that will determine how we survive them. I've heard it said that when God wants to reveal Himself to you on another level, He would consistently create or allow someone or something to make a crisis in your life. Learn to recognize and embrace them. I am convinced that God was allowing me to get to know Him on a whole other level by the frequency and relationship of my losses because five months after I lost my husband, I lost my youngest brother as well. It was raining crises for me, I thought. But when we experience God on that other level, our crisis will no longer crush us under the burden of its weight.

When I look at some of my wedding pictures and videos, I see my brother, Paul with Cash and me, enjoying himself the entire time. I see that as a blessing from God to me. That was the last time I saw him happy. He once told me that he had had a dream where Jesus was knocking on a door, and he was on the other side. He said he didn't know what to do, so he asked me what he should do. I was pretty surprised that he would ask me that question. I thought, *Didn't he know?* He attended the same church I did growing up. It was he who went to a Christian school while I attended public schools. Surely my brother must know what to do. I reminded him of what Jesus said in Revelation 3:20: "Behold, I stand at the door, and knock: if any man hear my voice, and open the door, I will come in to him." I said to him, "Open the door." I don't know if he ever did, though. Only time will tell.

Somewhere between January 3, 2016, and May 29, 2018, I had changed. I am still growing in my faith. I'm developing a closer walk with God. By doing so, I am learning to trust Him even when things are not as I want them or pray for them to be. When my middle sister died, it brought out a lot of anger and mistrust toward God in me. I needed peace from Jehovah-Shalom, and God brought me peace. When my oldest sister, my mother, and my husband were about to die from their illnesses, they needed Jehovah-Rapha, the God who heals, but they got Jehovah-Shalom, the God of peace. Not what I had prayed for, but that's what I got—a God who gave them peace in their darkest hour.

The knowledge of that is what brings the peace back to me. William J Kirkpatrick wrote, "'Tis so sweet to trust in Jesus, just to take Him at His word: just to rest upon His promise: just to know, Thus saith the Lord. Jesus, Jesus how I trust Him, how I've proved Him o'er and o'er, Jesus, Jesus, precious Jesus! O for grace to trust Him more." Thank God I had peace. I just need to trust Jesus more.

BLESSED ASSURANCE

Would to God that my husband was still here. I had not known such loneliness before. There is not a day that goes by when I don't think of him and smile. The tears still come, but I thank God that I can smile despite the tears. The longing in my heart to see him again weighs heavy on my soul. It brings me to a place daily where there is nothing left but hope in God. And Jehovah El Roi, the God who sees me, knows my pain. That is why He's with me, always comforting me through His Holy Spirit. He will gladly do the same for you in your pain.

Right now, I don't understand this. I don't understand this because I was focusing on healing for my husband. I was only focused on the life we both planned together. But the omniscient God who knows the end from the beginning, Jehovah Jireh, the God who provides, had already orchestrated a plan for the redemption of man. It is that God who always has a resurrection on His mind.

As I lie in the bed that I once shared with my husband, I'm reminded by the absence of his presence how my life has changed forever. All around me, things go on for others as before. They go on because they must. They go on because my husband's death did not affect them personally as it did me. That is not to say that no one cared; it is simply that his life was not an everyday part of theirs.

I choose to smile every time I think of him. I smile when I remember his captivating smile. I smile when I remember his electrifying personality. I smile when I remember that even in his darkest hours, his quiet strength was still there for me. I smile when I remember how he loved me. Most of all, I smile because I trust God's promise of the resurrection. I know I will see him again. Hallelujah—thank You, Jesus.

I've learned that as normal and healthy as tears are, nothing beats a smile when you have joy inside. So I smile often and allow it to unbind the chains of the pain I carry. While I have not forgotten any of the bad times, I simply use the memory to fuel my remembrance of all the good times I had with my loved ones. I've learned to thank God for having those times to remember. My words can never fully convey the depth of gratitude I feel. In that single act of the marriage between my husband and myself, I've garnered just a tiny inkling of how much God loves me. But He loves me so much more than that.

It's inconceivable, I know, but I know He loves me more than words can say. It was that single act on Calvary that also proves my claim is right. My friend, He loves you just as much! Unlike the game of poker, God is not hiding His hand, waiting for us to show ours first. He has freely shown us His hand. Not only did He show us, He told us first back in the garden of Eden. In the fullness of time, He played His best card, and nothing that we can bring to the table will ever be able to beat it.

He's preparing an eternal home for my loved ones and me. It can be your home as well if you choose. Like God, is there anything you won't do for love? By now, it should come as no surprise to you that I believe in the resurrection. The thought of seeing my loved ones again steadies me on my journey. The sting of death is real, but it's not lasting. Nevertheless, it does not lessen the blow when it claims the life of a loved one. Neither does it when it knocks at our very own door. Be of great cheer, my friend, for hope does much abound. While death may be the end of our story for life on this earth, it will ring in the beginning of our new life to come.

God's plan of redemption was put into action the moment sin entered the world. It was a plan that required the blood of the innocent Jesus. This plan would save humanity and restore what Adam had lost. Finding comfort daily in God's word is my saving grace. Just allowing myself to start each day asking for the strength to get through that one day makes getting through that one day possible. Having daily talks with God, who is my strength, asking Him to guide my footsteps lest I go astray, has made such a difference in my life.

I have heard some say that my loved ones are in a better place, or they're in heaven looking down on me. Allow me to disagree wholeheartedly. I assume that the comments are meant to suggest that they are in heaven. But that cannot be true because Jesus has not yet returned; therefore, there has been no resurrection. If there has been no resurrection, then who is it that we know personally that is in heaven? I choose to believe the words of Jesus Himself, that He will return for His people, and every eye will see Him. I'm excitedly looking forward to beholding His glory.

BEYOND THE GRAVE

I now know that through all of my pain and losses, I've learned to trust that Jesus understands the painful sense of loss we feel when we lose a loved one. He understands the burden we carry from the regrets we sometimes feel. Jesus understands the all-consuming aloneness we're bound to feel. And I know He understands our helplessness.

I know this because when I think about Jesus's death on Calvary's cross, I imagine Him looking back and forward in time, seeing all of our trials and tribulations, seeing the pain they would cause, and then taking all of that pain upon Himself. I imagine Him looking from the cross to His resurrection and from His resurrection to His second coming, and seeing how glorious it will be. I also imagine Jesus seeing that the price He paid was worth it. Then, I imagine His beautiful smile—a smile that lights the world. And if I can imagine this, then I can say with hope and great confidence that death or dying is not the end because Jesus conquered death. It has been swallowed up in victory.

> O death, where is thy sting? O grave, where is thy victory? (1 Corinthians 15:55)

We all must grieve the loss of our loved ones. Jesus Himself wept when Lazarus died. He did not weep because of hopelessness or helplessness, Jesus wept because He understood Mary and Martha's pain due to the loss of their brother.

In our grieving however, let us remember that hope is not lost when death takes us away. Hope is not lost, because that same Jesus who wept at Lazarus's death also raised him from the dead as an example of what was to be at His second coming. Again, I believe that some of my greatest strengths came when I focused on the resurrection.

> But I would not have you be ignorant brethren, concerning them which are asleep, that ye sorrow not, even as others which have no hope. For if we believe that Jesus died and rose again, even so them also which sleep in Jesus will God bring with Him. For this we say unto you by the word of the Lord that we who are alive and remain unto the coming of the Lord shall not prevent them which are asleep. For the Lord himself shall descend from heaven with a shout, with the voice of the archangel, and with the trump of God; and the dead in Christ shall rise first. (1 Thessalonians 4:13–16)

Please close your eyes with me and allow the following words to breathe hope into your soul.

> Then we which are alive and remain shall be caught up together with them in the clouds, to meet the Lord in the air: and so shall we ever be with the Lord. Wherefore comfort one another with these words. (1 Thessalonians 4:17–18)

And so I say to all of you that if we believe that God is who He says He is—if we believe that Jesus Christ died and rose from the dead—if we believe that Jesus is coming back for His people, we cannot stay where we are. We cannot remain in a state of pain, heartache, and confusion when we lose a loved one. We cannot remain in a state of fear. We cannot stay in a state of brokenness. We cannot remain in a state of hopelessness. We cannot, and we must not.

Going through the pain is a part of the natural healing process.

But God has assured us that brighter days are coming. Remember what God said in Jeremiah 29:11:

> "For I know the plans I have for you," declares the
> Lord, "plans to prosper and not to harm you, plans to
> give you hope and a future."

That future is with Him. When adversity comes our way through the loss of loved ones, we should grieve, but not despair. We must realize that God sometimes allows unwanted things to happen to test us. He allows them to grow our faith and strengthen our relationship with Him. Remember, if He allows it, He's also made ways for you to get through it victoriously.

Often we're quick to talk about the goodness of God when others are having difficulties in their lives. We're quick to tell others to have faith and that all things work together for good. We're quick to say, "I'll pray for you." When our turn comes and we're tested, God is looking on with all of heaven to see if we can now walk the talk. Just as the apostle Paul said in Romans 8:38–39 (NKJV), "'I am persuaded that neither death nor life, nor angels nor principalities nor powers, nor things present nor things to come, nor height nor depth, nor any other created thing, shall be able to separate us from the love of God which is in Christ Jesus our Lord." Oh yes, my friend, we have a glorious future to look forward to. Hold that hope in your heart. Keep it there, for your reward will soon come.

> Behold, I come quickly; and my reward is with me,
> to give every man according as his work shall be.
> (Revelation 22:12)

OUR NEW HOME

THE NEW JERUSALEM

There are no words more beautiful to describe our eternal home than those found in Revelation chapters 21 and 22.

> And I saw a new heaven and a new earth: for the first heaven and the first earth were passed away; and there was no more sea. And I, John, saw the holy city, new Jerusalem, coming down from God out of heaven, prepared as a bride adorned for her husband. And I heard a great voice out of heaven saying, Behold, the tabernacle of God is with men, and he will dwell with them, and they shall be his people, and God himself shall be with them, and be their God. And God shall wipe away all tears from their eyes; and there shall be no more death, neither sorrow, nor crying, neither shall there be any more pain: for the former things are passed away. ... He that overcometh shall inherit all things; and I will be his God, and he shall be my son. ... And there came unto me one of the seven angels which had the seven vials full of the seven last plagues, and talked with me, saying, Come hither, I will shew thee the bride, the Lamb's wife. And he carried me away in the spirit to a great and high mountain, and shewed me that great city, the holy Jerusalem, descending out of Heaven from

God, having the glory of God: and her light was like unto a stone most precious, even like a jasper stone, clear as crystal; and had a wall great and high, and had twelve gates, and at the gates twelve angels, and names written thereon, which are the names of the twelve tribes of the children of Israel: on the east three gates; on the north three gates; on the south three gates; and on the west three gates. And the wall of the city had twelve foundations, and in them the names of the twelve apostles of the Lamb. And he that talked with me had a golden reed to measure the city, and the gates thereof, and the wall thereof. And the city lieth foursquare, and the length is as large as the breadth: and he measured the city with the reed, twelve thousand furlongs. The length and the breadth and the height of it are equal. And he measured the wall thereof, an hundred and forty and four cubits, according to the measure of a man, that is, of the angel. And the building of the wall of it was of jasper: and the city was pure gold, like unto clear glass. And the foundations of the wall of the city were garnished with all manner of precious stones. The first foundation was jasper; the second, sapphire; the third, a chalcedony; the fourth, an emerald; the fifth, sardonyx; the sixth, sardius; the seventh, chrysolyte; the eighth, beryl; the ninth, a topaz; the tenth, a chrysoprasus; the eleventh, a jacinth; the twelfth, an amethyst. And the twelve gates were twelve pearls: every several gate was of one pearl: and the street of the city was pure gold, as it were transparent glass. And I saw no temple therein: for the Lord God Almighty and the Lamb are the temple of it. And the city had no need of the sun, neither of the moon, to shine in it: for the glory of God did lighten it, and the Lamb is the light thereof. And the nations of them which are saved shall walk in the light of it: and the kings of the earth do bring their glory and honor into it. And the gates of it shall not be shut at all by day: for there shall be no night there. And they shall bring the glory and honor of the nations into it. And there shall in no wise enter into it any thing that defileth, neither whatsoever worketh abomination, or maketh a lie: but they which are written in the Lamb's book of life. And he showed me a pure river of water of life, clear as crystal, proceeding out of the throne of God and of the Lamb. In the midst of the street of it, and on either side of the river, was there the tree of life, which bare twelve manner of fruits, and yielded her fruit every month: and the leaves of the tree were for the healing of the nations. And there shall be no more curse: but the throne of God and of the Lamb shall be in it; and his servants shall serve him: and they shall see his face; and his name shall be in their foreheads. And there shall be no night there; and they need no candle, neither light of the sun; for the Lord God giveth them light: and they shall reign forever and ever. (Revelation 21:1–22:5)

THE REVELATION

Can you see it? Do you long to live in that eternal home? As I told you in the beginning, Jesus says to us in John 14:1–3, "Let not your heart be troubled: ye believe in God, Believe also in me. In my Father's house are many mansions: if it were not so, I would have told you. I go to prepare a place for you. And if I go and prepare a place for you, I will come again, and receive you unto myself; that where I am, there ye may be also." No matter how much it hurts now when we lose a loved one, remember that one day, God will wipe away all tears from our eyes; and there shall be no more death, neither sorrow nor crying; neither shall there be any more pain: for the former things will be wiped away. (Revelation 21:4)

My prayer is that you, my brothers and sisters in Christ, have found comfort, confidence, and hope. Not in my words, but rather the comfort that can only come from the power of the living God through His Holy Spirit. The power over death is Christ's alone. No, my friend, death is not the end for those who die in Christ. It is merely the last enemy we must face before the judgment. We can rest assured that all those who die in Jesus Christ not only rest from their labor but are also guaranteed a place in heaven. The marvelous hope and blessed assurance that we all have, though the dead have no more part in this life, is that all those who sleep in our Lord Jesus Christ are resting on the Edge of Eternity.

Jesus Paid It All

I hear the Savior say,
"Thy strength indeed is small;
Child of weakness, watch and pray,
Find in Me thine all in all."

When from my dying bed
My ransomed soul shall rise,
"Jesus died my soul to save,"
Shall rend the vaulted skies.

And when before the throne
I stand in Him complete,
I'll lay my trophies down,
All down at Jesus' feet.

Jesus paid it all,
All to Him I owe;
Sin had left a crimson stain,
He washed it white as snow.

—Elvina Hall

A Light Still Burning

With a head held high and arms open wide,
I give thanks for all that I am
For the beat of my heart, for the love of my
life, that kept my heart still yearning
For brighter days and glorious nights.
I am a light still burning
With a quiet smile for days gone by, a wish carried off in the wind
With heartfelt prayers, unwavering faith,
yet still my heart is yearning
For brighter days and glorious nights.
I am a light still burning
I shine from within to those who know me, my
journey not yet done
I've lived, I've loved, perhaps done it all,
and yet my heart is still yearning
For brighter days for glorious nights.
I am a light still burning.

—Valencia McMahon

SCRIPTURES FOR COMFORT

And God shall wipe away all tears from their eyes; and there shall be no more death, neither sorrow, nor crying, neither shall there be any more pain: for the former things are passed away. (Revelation 21:4)

My flesh and my heart fail; but God is the strength of my heart and my portion forever. … But it is good for me to draw near to God; I have put my trust in the Lord God that I may declare all His works. (Psalm 73:26, 28)

Let not your heart be troubled; you believe in God, believe also in me. In my Father's house are many mansions; if it were not so I would have told you. I go to prepare a place for you. And if I go to prepare a place for you, I will come again and receive you unto myself; that where I am, there you may be also. (John 14:1–3)

Psalm 119:50
This is my comfort in my affliction: for thy word hath quickened me. (Psalm 119:50)

For the Lord will not cast off forever: but though he cause grief, yet will he have compassion according to the multitude of his mercies. For He doth not afflict willingly nor grieve the children of men. (Lamentations 3:31–33)

For this we say unto you by the word of the Lord, that we which are alive and remain unto the coming of the Lord shall not prevent them which are asleep. For the Lord himself shall descend from heaven with a shout, with the voice of the archangel, and with the trump of God: and the dead in Christ shall rise first. (1 Thessalonians 4:15–16)

For God so loved the world that He gave His only begotten Son, that whoever believes in Him should not perish but have everlasting life. (John 3:16 NKJV)

For our light and momentary troubles are achieving for us an eternal glory that far outweighs them all. (2 Corinthians 4:17 NIV)

And this is life eternal, that they might know thee the only true God, and Jesus Christ, whom thou hast sent. (John 17:3)

And if children, then heirs—heirs of God and joint heirs with Christ, if indeed we suffer with Him, that we may also be glorified together. For I consider that the sufferings of this present time are not worthy to be compared with the glory, which shall be revealed in us. (Romans 8:17–18)

MESSAGES OF HOPE

To my dear readers, I sincerely thank you for reading this book. I hope that you've realized that you are not alone. Sadly, it is true that in our lives, we all will suffer pain and grief. Sometimes those emotions can be quite unbearable. Your heart may feel as if the pain will never go away. Your very spirit can feel weakened by the loss. At times like these, your faith in God may take a blow as well. The million-dollar question "Why does God allow this?" now comes into play. You may even question your own faith. I know I did.

The good news is that it's okay. God can handle our questions, but we must know that He cares deeply for us—for you and for me. He feels our pain and grieves when we grieve. The simple fact is that we are not always given answers to the whys. Take comfort instead in the fact that God knows our sorrows and will soon put an end to them.

The cross of Calvary showed the world the height, the depth, and the breadth of God's love for His creation. Remember, God gave His only Son to die for a fallen human race. Surely you must know that as God grieved for His Son, He grieves for the human race. There are times when my heart is heavy when I think about God giving up His all to save me and those I love. There are also times when I stand in awe as I think about how Jesus lovingly died for me. He did not want to die on a cross, but He did—for me. He died for you too.

How is it then that we are not willing in turn to lose what we love? Isn't His resurrection proof that He will bring His children home as He promised? Jesus has gone to prepare a place for you and me where pain and death will no longer exist. It is in the new heaven and new earth where we will reunite with our loved ones who died in Christ. I believe in my heart that He will keep His promise; I hope you do too, because the minute that you do, your life will never be the same. And so I challenge you in the midst of your pain and grief to turn your eyes upon Jesus. Look full in His wonderful face, and the things of this earth will grow strangely dim in the light of His glory and grace. My brothers and sisters in Christ, I'll see you in heaven.

Valencia

Edge of Eternity

I can do all things through Christ who strengthens me.
—Philippians 4:13 (NKJV)

Have I not commanded you? Be strong and courageous.
Do not be frightened, and do not be dismayed, for the
Lord your God is with you wherever you go.
—Joshua 1:9 (ESV)

For God so loved the world, that he gave his only
begotten Son, that whosoever believeth in him
should not perish, but have everlasting life
—John 3:16

Printed in the United States
by Baker & Taylor Publisher Services